DR. COLBERT'S
KETO ZONE DIET

DR. COLBERT'S
KETO ZONE DIET

Burn Fat, Balance Appetite
Hormones, and Lose Weight

DON COLBERT, MD

WORTHY®
PUBLISHING

Published by Worthy Books, an imprint of Worthy Publishing Group, a division of Worthy Media, Inc., One Franklin Park, 6100 Tower Circle, Suite 210, Franklin, TN 37067.

WORTHY is a registered trademark of Worthy Media, Inc.

HELPING PEOPLE EXPERIENCE THE HEART OF GOD

eBook available wherever digital books are sold.

Library of Congress Cataloging-in-Publication Data

Names: Colbert, Don, author.
Title: Keto zone diet : burn fat, balance hormones, and lose weight / Don
  Colbert, M.D.
Description: Franklin, TN : Worthy, [2017]
Identifiers: LCCN 2017020127 | ISBN 9781683970248 (hardback)
Subjects: LCSH: Ketogenic diet. | Reducing diets. | BISAC: HEALTH & FITNESS /
  Nutrition.
Classification: LCC RC374.K46 C65 2017 | DDC 613.2/5--dc23
LC record available at https://lccn.loc.gov/2017020127

Unless otherwise noted, Scripture is taken from the New King James Version®. Copyright © 1982 by Thomas Nelson. Used by permission. All rights reserved. | Scripture quotations marked KJV are taken from the King James Version of the Bible. Public domain.

Medical Disclaimer: *Because each individual is different and has particular dietary needs or restrictions, the dieting and nutritional information provided in this book does not constitute professional advice and is not a substitute for expert medical advice. Individuals should always check with a doctor before undertaking a dieting, weight loss, or exercise regimen and should continue only under a doctor's supervision. While we provide the advice and information in this book in the hopes of helping individuals improve their overall health, multiple factors influence a person's results, and individual results may vary. When a doctor's advice to a particular individual conflicts with advice provided in this book, that individual should always follow the doctor's advice. Patients should not stop taking any of their medications without the consultation of their physician.*

For foreign and subsidiary rights, contact rights@worthypublishing.com

Published in association with Ted Squires Agency, Nashville, Tennessee

ISBN: 978-1-68397-024-8 (Hardcover)
ISBN: 978-1-68397-254-9 (Special Edition Hardcover)

Cover Design: Marc Whitaker, MTW Designs
Cover photo: istock.com 680547462; AlexRaths
Graphs and Graphics: Abraham Mast

Printed in the United States of America
17 18 19 20 21 LBM 8 7 6 5 4 3 2

This book is dedicated to my dear friends Kenneth and Gloria Copeland, as well Kenneth Copeland Ministries (KCM) and all KCM partners.

Brother Copeland has been a spiritual father to me, and I am very grateful to him for his continual guidance. He has taught me much about faith, as well as guarding my tongue and watching my words, which has helped tremendously in my walk of faith.

I pray that this book will enable you to walk in divine health as you gain greater knowledge, wisdom, and understanding of these breakthrough dietary principles.

After all, we agree on this:

Happy is the man who finds wisdom,
And the man who gains understanding;
For her proceeds are better than the profits of silver,
And her gain than fine gold.
She is more precious than rubies,
And all the things you may desire cannot compare with her.
Length of days is in her right hand,
In her left hand riches and honor.
—Proverbs 3:13–16

We have already been promised wisdom by James the brother of Jesus, who wrote:

If any of you lacks wisdom, let him ask of God, who gives to all liberally and without reproach, and it will be given to him.
—James 1:5

As we know, faith without works is dead. It is the application of these life principles that will enable your health to be renewed so that you can joyfully declare:

Bless the Lord, O my soul;
And all that is within me, bless His holy name!
Bless the Lord, O my soul,
And forget not all His benefits:
Who forgives all your iniquities,
Who heals all your diseases,
Who redeems your life from destruction,
Who crowns you with lovingkindness and tender mercies,
Who satisfies your mouth with good things
So that your youth is renewed like the eagle's.
—Psalm 103:1–5

CONTENTS

PROLOGUE

BROTHER KENNETH COPELAND and his wife, Gloria, first came to see me back in 2002. I was amazed to see they were both in excellent health and on no medications. They were only taking nutritional supplements.

After spending about three hours with me, I then had them see my nutritional counselor, who ran them through a computerized nutritional assessment. When Kenneth walked into her room, his eyes got real big and he shouted, "Praise God!" He then explained that his mother had been a practicing chiropractor and she had used a much earlier version of the machine I had. It had proven to be a help with many people, and he felt at home in my offices after seeing the same machine.

It was during my first encounter with Brother Copeland as a patient that he began to rub off on me. As we chatted, I began to see that he watches every word that comes out of his mouth very carefully. What's more, he also watches every word coming out of my mouth!

If I had a tiny amount of unbelief or doubt in anything I said, Kenneth would reply, "Dr. Colbert, would you please restate what you just said?" I would repeat it, and he would then say, "No, don't repeat it *that* way, but say what you said without any doubt or unbelief."

"Oh, sorry, Brother Copeland," I replied, trying to apologize for what I had said.

He replied rather loudly, "No, you are not sorry! Sorry means a sorry-no-good-person, and you are not a sorry-no-good-person."

For me, that was my initial lesson in guarding my tongue and speaking every word without doubt or unbelief!

Since then, I have had plenty of time to practice my faith conversations without doubt or unbelief. About every six months or so, when Kenneth and Gloria would come to see me, I knew that every word that proceeded out of my mouth had to be in agreement with God's Word and had to have no doubt or unbelief attached to it.

Because of Brother Copeland's guidance, when I would occasionally start down a doubt trail in our conversation, I would abruptly stop myself and say, "Let me rephrase that statement," and start again, removing the doubt and unbelief.

And by the way, I never said, "Oh, sorry" again. I knew what it meant and applied that truth to my life and with every conversation I had with patients.

Years later, Kenneth told me how he had overcome eating sugar and drinking excessive amounts of coffee. He explained how he used to drink coffee by the pot rather than by the cup. He also loved sugar and anything containing sugar.

One day the Lord was dealing with Kenneth about his diet, and Kenneth felt led to lay both sugar and coffee on the altar. He put a cup of coffee and a little bowl of sugar on the table, and then he took communion. Afterward, he prayed and pushed both the sugar and coffee away from him and declared, "I have no further need of you."

Kenneth has not had coffee or sugar since, and that was more than forty years ago! His physical health and mental acuity have no doubt benefited from that choice made so many years ago.

Some time after hearing this story from Brother Copeland, I had a young pastor come to my office. He had a big church with more than a thousand members on two separate campuses, but he came to me because he was tired, dejected, burned out, and had lost his passion for the gospel. In talking to him, I learned he was not even close to his goal of growing his church that he had set for himself ten years earlier. He felt like a failure, even though he was very successful as a pastor.

The young pastor was only forty years old, yet he was very tired, did not sleep well at night, and was getting up two to three times a night to urinate. The last part was a tell-tale sign. Sure enough, after checking his blood sugar levels, I told him he was a type 2 diabetic and would need to give up sugar in order to reverse the diabetes.

I thought he would be ecstatic to learn that he could reverse his type 2 diabetes simply by changing his eating habits. Instead, he looked even more sad, like he had lost his best friend. I added, "Thank God it's not cancer or heart disease. It's just type 2 diabetes, and it's easy to reverse with diet alone!"

He explained that the foods he loved and craved the most were foods packed with sugars. Interestingly, for so many of my patients, the foods they crave and enjoy the most are usually the very foods that are inviting disease into their bodies. For the young pastor, sugar had become his comforter, his Holy Ghost substitute, and it was wreaking havoc in his body.

The young pastor chose to follow my dietary program. I am confident, as I have seen with many other patients, that in three to four short months, his type 2 diabetes will be reversed.

You, too, can overcome a sugar addiction. If you are addicted to sugar, breakthrough is not far away! It all starts with a desire to give up sugar and to confess every day that the Holy Spirit will be your comforter.

After all, the Holy Spirit lives inside of you. You are more than a conqueror through Him. You can and will overcome and conquer sugar cravings!

> Yet in all these things we are more than conquerors through Him who loved us.
> —Romans 8:37

Make that declaration and, as Brother Copeland did, set aside a time to take communion. Place your favorite sugar treat right in front of you. After praying and taking communion, push the sugary treat away from you and say, "I have no further need of you."

Remember to say your confessions daily, declaring that sugar is no longer your comforter but that the Holy Spirit is, that you can do this through Jesus, and other confessions that strengthen your heart and mind.

After all, if we cannot resist a donut, a cookie, or a bowl of ice cream, how are we going to resist the devil, cancer, heart disease, diabetes, Alzheimer's, or any of the other thirty-five major diseases?

Temperance, which is an old-fashioned word for self-control, is one of the fruits of the Spirit.

> But the fruit of the Spirit is love, joy, peace, longsuffering, gentleness, goodness, faith, meekness, temperance: against such there is no law.
> —Galatians 5:22–23 KJV

Temperance is a fruit that is grown by consistently making the right choices. While the well-known Gifts of the Spirit are given to us by God, temperance is grown by you and your choices. You cannot receive temperance by prayer, the laying on of hands, or by impartation. It only comes by consistently making the right choices. It is a fruit that is cultivated and grown, and only then it is enjoyed.

Choosing to eat sugar actually invites most every disease into the body. When Adam and Eve sinned, they infected the entire human race with the sin nature. Unfortunately, most Christians are also choosing sugar on a daily basis, with the result being the unknowing invitation of most every deadly disease into their body and mind.

We all know this truth:

> Do not be deceived, God is not mocked; for whatever a man sows, that he will also reap. For he who sows to his flesh will of the flesh reap corruption, but he who sows to the Spirit will of the Spirit reap everlasting life.
> —Galatians 6:7–8

According to *Strong's Exhaustive Concordance of the Bible*, this "corruption" that we reap into our flesh means to: decay, destroy, perish. That is exactly the eventual course of cancer, Alzheimer's, diabetes, heart disease, autoimmune disease, and many other diseases if left unchecked!

The restoration of your health starts with the right diet. You must begin with removing the foods that fuel disease. The ketogenic diet is the diet that Brother Copeland told me he would follow for the rest of his life because it closes the door on most diseases.

I strongly believe we are now living in the end times. I have decided that I'm going to devote the rest of my life to not treat disease with medication but to prevent and reverse disease by teaching patients the principles that are in this book.

It all starts with the right diet, and that is what this book is all about.

Imagine living in the end times—the most exciting time in human history—strong, healthy, full of energy, resistant to every disease, and able to preach the gospel with passion, energy, and being full of the Holy Ghost. It doesn't get any better than that!

Join me, Kenneth, and Gloria in the lifestyle that makes you stronger, prevents disease, and helps you lose weight. It is by far, in my opinion, the healthiest lifestyle in the world!

Finally, let me ask you one last question: Can you now resist a donut, cookie, or any other sugar?

Of course you can!

ACKNOWLEDGMENTS

THIS BEING A UNIQUE BOOK, one that has so much potential to change our lives, homes, futures, pocketbooks, communities, and world, I wanted to begin with a few special acknowledgments (confessions, really) that I hope will help you.

I acknowledge:

- I used to recommend the usual high-carb, low-fat diet to my patients.
- I used to prescribe the normal statin drugs to lower my patients' cholesterol.
- I used to fear fat.
- I used to suffer from psoriasis over most of my body, and did so for more than twelve years.
- I used to have very little in the line of defense against the disease that killed my father: Alzheimer's.

However, that is no longer the case. Now, I see food and use food for what it can be . . . the best medicine in the world for everything that ails us.

From head to toe, the results have been astounding!

INTRODUCTION

LOSING WEIGHT, getting healthy, and staying fit come down to a belief system. That is because we all choose to do whatever we believe in. Obviously, believing that eating donuts is a valid weight-loss strategy does not make it so, no matter how much we hope it to be true. The point is, our choices directly affect our actions and are influenced by what we believe. We choose to do whatever we believe in.

The challenge is, what do you do when the rules change?

Take eggs for example. For decades, we were taught that egg yolks were bad for us because they contain cholesterol. Like many people, I would eat one yolk and three egg whites, and I recommended that to my patients. After all, cholesterol is bad, right?

Well, things change.

According to the 2015 Dietary Guidelines for Americans published by the Office of Disease Prevention and Health Promotion, it is now okay to eat the whole egg.[1] In fact, you can now eat as many whole eggs as you want. The rules changed!

We are so used to eggs being "bad guys" that now we are faced with a choice: believe what we were taught since the 1950s or accept the new reality that whole eggs are in fact healthy.

What to do? What to believe? Naturally, what you choose to believe will be your course of action.

This eggs-are-now-healthy breakthrough is just one of countless examples. What is happening on a much bigger scale is that the much-touted high-carb, low-fat "healthy" lifestyle is springing leaks. Holes are appearing in this rusty metal tub of a belief system. The ship is sinking. And it is time to abandon ship as quickly as you can.

It is a paradigm shift, and it is happening now. It will take time for new breakthroughs to be tested and retested, and even more time for the public to be informed through the slow-to-change medical community and government agencies.

One of my professors in medical school explained that in about ten years, half of what we were being taught would be outdated and pretty much of no value. He noted, "The problem is we don't know which half that is."

Eventually, though, public opinion will shift. People will understand and accept the new paradigm, and then they will choose to take action. Unfortunately, that will take a very long time, and time is a commodity many of us do not have.

For years I have treated patients who suffered from advanced cancers, obesity, type 2 diabetes, heart disease, mental illness, and much more. They needed help yesterday so they could be on the road to healing today. They were desperate, and they had no time to wait!

Thankfully, we already have sufficient data, research, studies, and real-life examples to know we are going in the right direction. What is more, many of my patients—who were written off by their own doctors—are alive and well today.

The answer was not a pill, medication, pharmaceutical drug, or surgery. The answer was a nutritional one completely based on the food we eat.

In a nutshell, this diet is low-carb, high-fat, and moderate protein. It is incredibly healthy, and not only does it work to cure or manage disease, it is the best weight-loss method in the world.

I call it the Keto Zone diet.

When you are in the Keto Zone, extra weight falls off. I've seen people lose as much as a pound per day, but one to two pounds per week is more common, perhaps three pounds with daily exercise. In a few weeks or months, the results are cumulative and astounding.

Wait a minute, you might be thinking. *Did you just say this was a high-fat diet? How can fat be healthy?*

To clarify, the Keto Zone diet is a purposeful combination of reduced carbs, increased healthy fats, and a moderate amount of healthy proteins. Yes, it is high-fat, but it is also (and very importantly) low-carb and moderate-protein. These elements go together to create a body that is satisfied, alert, happy, and fat-burning.

When it comes to fats, not all are bad for you. However, we have been taught for so long that fats are bad that we have a very real and tangible fear of fat. And why not? The message from most doctors, food guidelines, trends magazines, and every other "authority" in life tells us in big bold letters that fat is BAD.

In truth, healthy fats are good. They are necessary. They will help you lose weight. And no, they will not make you fat, clog your arteries, or cause you to drop dead.

The Keto Zone diet works. It also cures or manages countless diseases.

If you are ready for that, then come on. A new life awaits!

This book is divided into three main parts:

Part One: What the Keto Zone diet is, the science and history behind it, and the reasons why it is so effective for weight loss and fighting diseases. The benefits of the Keto Zone diet are off the charts!

Part Two: Why the Keto Zone diet works, why each piece of the puzzle goes together so well, and why the Keto Zone diet is, indeed, the best and healthiest way to lose weight.

Part Three: The simple steps to implement the Keto Zone diet and exactly what it takes to get you into the fat-burning zone. This includes practical shopping guides, step-by-step instructions, and menu plans.

I recommend that you read part one and part two before plunging into the diet and menus, as these sections answer many questions, empower you, and give you unstoppable confidence moving forward. But if you are ready to jump in, then feel free to move directly to part three. That is where action and change take place.

The Keto Zone diet works, and in more ways than one. I have had literally thousands of patients on this diet, and the positive results are amazing, life-changing, and in some cases unbelievable.

On a personal note, I am incredibly excited about my second book with Worthy. As a Christian first and medical doctor second, my beliefs fall right in line with my publisher's mission statement: "Helping people experience the heart of God." My desire is that you experience a healthy lifestyle that allows you to not only enjoy life to the fullest, but to also love God and serve Him to the best of your ability. May the Keto Zone diet give you the hope you've been searching for. To your health!

PART ONE

What the Keto Zone Diet Is

What the Keto Zone diet is, the science and history behind it, and the reasons why it is so effective for weight loss and fighting diseases. The benefits of the Keto Zone diet are off the charts!

CHAPTER ONE
MEETING A REAL NEED

THE WIFE WAS CONFUSED, but the husband was terrified. I could see it in his eyes. This was because his wife of more than thirty years had just been diagnosed with early dementia.

With her back against the wall, so to speak, the couple was willing to try pretty much anything. Believe it or not, mild dementia in its early stages is usually pretty easy to treat and even cure, and within six months, she had a clean bill of health. Her dementia was completely gone.

And she had lost almost forty pounds.

And she looked great, was full of life, and had a sparkle in her eye.

And her husband could smile again!

What was the secret? It is no secret at all. She went on a revised ketogenic diet that I call the Keto Zone diet. As a direct result, she got her life back. Today, years later, I am pleased to report that she is still doing well.

WHAT IS THIS DIET?

I have been practicing medicine for more than thirty years. About twenty years ago, something strange started to happen. People with incurable, inoperable, late-stage cancers began showing up at my office.

They all needed help, but I was not a cancer specialist. I had found a way to beat the psoriasis (my own twelve-year battle that was incredibly expensive, not to mention time-consuming) that had plagued me, but I did not feel qualified to treat these cancer patients adequately. I wanted to help, and even more, I wanted to improve and prolong their lives, but I knew what I knew, and it was not enough. There had to be an answer. There always is. Many of these patients were past the point where surgery, chemotherapy, radiation, or some other form of traditional cancer treatment would help.

Out of an intense desire to help, mixed with the humble reality that I needed to learn more, I went on a journey to find answers that would allow my patients not only to survive but to thrive as well.

Every continuing education class that was remotely related to cancer, nutrition, diet, lifestyle, and longevity went on my must-attend list. I firmly believed the answer was a nutritional one. That was true for my psoriasis, and I not only knew the stats on such things as obesity, heart disease, diabetes, and mental illness, I saw those stats walk through my office door every single day.

> ## IT'S A FACT
>
> We have been told so many times that carbohydrates are good and fats are bad that we *believe* it to be a fact.

The national rapid rise in preventable diseases wreaking havoc on so many lives was not new to me. I saw it firsthand. Part of the problem had to do with the foods we ate. That much I knew.

Along the way, I studied nutritional and preventative medicine, antiaging therapies, and integrative cancer therapy. I visited cancer treatment centers and listened to specialists from all around the world present their best and most recent findings on alternative and nutritional therapy for cancer. In all, I cannot tell you how many seminars I attended (my wife probably could), but after several years of training and then coming back and working with my patients, I was convinced there was no silver bullet. There was no miracle cure.

But I kept returning to food. I was certain that the answer for my cancer patients, and the multitude of preventable diseases we are experiencing today, had to do with the food we ate. But even that is a pretty broad field.

During my fellowship in integrative cancer therapy, I asked the head instructor, "Is there any key nutritional therapy for cancer patients?"

He thought for a moment and replied, "The only major impactful thing is a ketogenic diet, but nobody can really follow that. Nobody can stick to it over the long term."

So there was an answer! There was a diet that actually could help reverse, manage, or even perhaps cure cancer. No doubt it would also work on other diseases if it was so effective with cancers. The only roadblock was that people lacked the stamina or motivation to stick with it.

I did not view that as a good enough reason to ignore the ketogenic diet. I knew from countless experiences that most cancer patients would do absolutely anything to live a little longer. When faced with death, our comforts and wants and preferences do not seem as important as they once were.

EXPLORING KETOGENIC DIETS

I made it my goal then to find out just what made the ketogenic diet so beneficial. Could it actually help my patients?

Back then, the word *ketogenic* was looked down upon. Dr. Robert Atkins, whom I had known for many years, was the biggest name associated with the ketogenic diet. His famous Atkins Diet had always seemed very unhealthy to me, but I was determined to study it further.

In time, I would go through countless books on the subject from experts who were medical doctors, dieticians, nutritionists, naturalists, and researchers. I investigated every premise inside the books. If it was important enough for authors to write it down, and it could be verified in some way, then it was worth considering.

Another filter that I ran every detail through was the reality of my own patients. Outrageous claims have a way of being brought down to earth when applied to the living and breathing patients in my office. I wanted this to work for them, both scientifically as well as practically.

I knew, for example, that cancers feed on sugars. Lowering or eliminating sugar intake had a direct effect on the cancer. The normal high-carb, low-fat diet of most people was simply feeding the cancers. That much I already knew.

What about cholesterol? I did not want to start my cancer patients on a low-carb, high-fat ketogenic diet that would blast their cholesterol levels through the roof and give them a heart attack. Some of my patients were dying of cancer, but I certainly did not want to speed up the process and have them die of heart disease.

What about fats? I had been taught that low-fat diets were better because fats were known to cause heart disease. But were fats really the cause? Some ketogenic diets recommend large amounts of bacon, lard, beef tallow, and fried foods. How could those be healthy? Amazingly, the diet actually helped people lose weight, which was the goal, but could the same results be achieved in a healthier manner? And would that benefit my cancer patients?

I also knew inflammation was the root cause of many sicknesses, including the psoriasis that I had battled for many years. For me it was certain foods that caused the inflammation, so it only stood to reason that many other illnesses were caused by inflammation from other foods we ate—maybe not directly but probably indirectly.

After much sifting, sorting, examining, measuring, verifying, researching, and dissecting, it was time to start introducing a modified version (a healthy version) of the ketogenic diet to my cancer patients. The patients I initially started on the modified ketogenic diet had advanced cancers (stages 3 and 4) and were much more likely to die of cancer than heart disease.

EXAMINING THE KETOGENIC DIET

The ketogenic diet seemed to be part of the answer. But I had a lot of questions, not to mention reservations and feelings of responsibility for my patients.

Mentally, I had my list of critical components that needed sufficient answers:

✓ Inflammation
✓ Cholesterol levels
✓ Fats
✓ Sugars
✓ Proteins

✓ Nutrients
✓ Starches
✓ Carbohydrates
✓ Medications
✓ Appetite hormones

I did my best to combine the best of everything I knew. I incorporated the research on nutrition, antiaging, the ketogenic diet, exercise, and natural cancer treatments all together.

I had been taking patients off gluten for years, not just because some are deathly allergic to it (as are celiac patients) or because gluten-free is a good trend to jump on, but rather because of the inflammation associated with gluten and especially the inflammation and disruption that it triggers in the GI tract where approximately two-thirds of the immune system is based.

Whether it is bread, cereal, pasta, crackers, or chips, these foods are not what they used to be. Today, grains like wheat, corn, oat, and rice are hybridized, crossbred, refined, and devoid of fiber and many other nutrients. Comparing today's processed grains to unrefined whole grains is almost like comparing an orange M&M to an actual orange. Not the same by any means!

I cannot tell you how many patients have shown immediate improvement after removing gluten from their diets. The ketogenic diet being low in carbohydrates was in line with that thinking.

Fats were another source of inflammation, but what about raising cholesterol levels and weight gain? I had noticed that fats controlled appetite and helped tame hunger, and I knew the body, principally the brain, could not thrive on a low-fat diet. Clearly, fats were a vital part of a healthy body, but how much fat? What types of fat? Was there an ideal ratio or combination of fats that would help with weight loss while at the same time protect against disease? Balance seemed to be a vital part of the whole equation.

The numbers of people diagnosed with Alzheimer's disease, type 2 diabetes, cancer, obesity, and heart disease have been increasing dramatically for years. Nothing seems to hold back these diseases, no matter how many medications are prescribed or how many suggested daily caloric intake revisions are made. Was much of this because we did not understand fats? If so, this lack of knowledge was literally killing us on a scale of millions per year.

Some of the foods recommended in ketogenic diets, such as excessive animal proteins and animal fats, might not be good for my advanced cancer patients. I was not worried about their cholesterol levels, because many of these stage 3 and 4 cancer patients usually had only a few months to a year to live. Nobody was checking their cholesterol levels anymore. It was irrelevant information.

> **IT'S A FACT**
>
> This is the fastest, easiest, and healthiest way to burn fat.

Yes, the ketogenic diets would help people burn fat and lose weight, but I would not put all of my patients on the exact same diet. The excessive animal fats and proteins were not the best for everyone. I had to adjust the diet some more for my cancer patients.

Appetite hormone levels were another part of the equation. They absolutely had to be managed. Obesity rates are a tell-tale sign that the hormones controlling appetite—those that signal "I'm full" or "I'm hungry"—are way out of whack. I have had obese patients tell me what they ate in one sitting only to conclude, "And when I finished I was still hungry."

If the ketogenic diet would bring the hormones related to appetite into balance, that would be a huge win for everyone battling obesity. The more I studied the ketogenic diet, the more I suspected these hormones would manage themselves once the patient was eating the proper foods and the correct balance of healthy fats.

That eventually led me to use the ketogenic diet for weight loss, a vital *need* for most people who are sick and an all-consuming *desire* for those who are overweight. The ketogenic diet became for my patients the fastest, easiest, and healthiest way to burn fat (especially belly fat) of all the other dietary programs I have used or recommended in the past thirty years of practicing medicine.

GIVING THE KETOGENIC DIET A TRY

Test after test, study upon study, bit by bit, I kept breaking down the parts of every ketogenic diet I could get my hands on. If I was going to prescribe it, I was going to understand it. I was going to know how it worked and why. And if I needed to tweak something for a patient or if a question arose, I needed to be able to respond accurately.

After much study and research, I felt it was time to begin implementing the ketogenic diet first with my advanced cancer patients. Admittedly, I still had some questions, but I knew that some questions were best answered by doing rather than by studying. Back to practicing medicine!

In case you are worried at this point, let me reassure you by explaining that I live on the ketogenic diet myself. I have a strong reason why: my dad died of Alzheimer's disease. I did genetic testing years ago on myself and found that I have the risk factor gene for Alzheimer's disease, which is the APOE4 gene. The risk of Alzheimer's is approximately ten times higher in those with the double variant of the gene.[2] Fortunately, I have the single variant of the gene, but still, I am going to do everything I can to prevent getting Alzheimer's. For me, staying on the ketogenic diet is a strong preventative measure. If I start eating a lot of sugars and carbohydrates, I could eventually develop Alzheimer's based on my genetic makeup. I do not want to go down that path. Instead, I control those genes by what I eat, and so can other people. For me, that is my compelling reason to stay in the Keto Zone, my version of a ketogenic diet.

As cancer patients came in for their exams, I recommended they follow a revised ketogenic diet. Even though a cancer specialist had told me "nobody can stick to a ketogenic diet," I'm telling you, a cancer patient with a one- or two-year life expectancy will do almost anything to live!

The patients followed the diet. It was low-carb, high-fat, and low- to moderate-protein. They carefully monitored their intake of carbohydrates, sugars, proteins, and fats. They gave up some of their comforts and habits, such as ice cream, diet sodas, breads, and alcohol. Together we created menu plans, and I had my patients write out their menus as well as their carb intake, calorie intake, and ketone status and e-mail me their meal plans each week.

One adjustment I made along the way was in the area of animal proteins. There was conflicting research at the time about excessive animal proteins being associated with cancers. I lowered animal protein intake for my patients, but now we know it is mainly the processed animal proteins (such as salami, sausage, pepperoni, hotdogs, and bacon) that are more closely associated with cancer, not so much the unprocessed meats.

Grass-fed meats, I later learned, are much healthier than grain-fed meats. In fact, grass-fed meats have more of all the healthy fats, minerals, and nutrients that our bodies need. A small fatty piece of steak, such as a rib eye from a grass-fed cow, is actually very healthy for you. Of course, we are talking about moderate amounts of protein, as we will discuss later.

It was not long before some of my cancer patients' lives changed dramatically. They got their energy back. They were happier. They lost belly fat. And most importantly, we were able to treat their end-stage cancer as a chronic disease. The diet slowed the cancer growth rates, and for some it was dramatic, by taking away what was fueling the cancer in the first place.

No, not every patient was able to bounce back. Many of the advanced cancer patients did die. The ketogenic diet did not cure their cancer, but for many it went from a highly invasive form to a more commensal state where instead of the cancer thriving, it shifted into more of a survival mode. In other words, for some, thanks to the ketogenic diet that limits sugar and starches, their cancer became much less aggressive. (Appendix D is for advanced-cancer patients.)

A great thing happened: many of my patients were living longer. I started checking their cholesterol levels. After all, they were on a low-carb, high-fat diet. And guess what? Their cholesterol levels usually improved. The HDL (good cholesterol) numbers usually went up, and the LDL (bad cholesterol) numbers typically went down. Here was further proof that the high-fat diet was not killing them.

Thanks to the ketogenic diet, we were also quenching inflammation, which was one of the reasons the diet worked against cancer.

As I focused on trying to help my patients beat or coexist with their cancer, I could not help but notice the other tremendous health benefits of the diet. People were losing weight, especially belly fat, which is the most inflammatory fat in our bodies, but it was much more than weight loss. As the years went by, the list of ailments, diseases, symptoms, and health markers positively affected by the ketogenic diet continued to grow. Here is what I found with most of my patients:

- Sleep disorders usually improved
- Migraines usually improved
- Type 2 diabetes usually improved or reversed

- ADHD and ADD usually improved
- Metabolic function usually restored
- Blood pressure usually lowered
- Fatty liver usually cured
- Irritable bowel syndrome (IBS) usually improved
- Dementia (mild to moderate) usually improved and for some cleared up
- Parkinson's (mild to moderate) usually improved and for some cleared up
- Chronic fatigue usually improved
- Energy levels significantly increased for many
- Mental illness, including schizophrenia and bipolar disorder, usually improved
- Fibromyalgia usually improved or cleared up
- Acne many times cleared up or improved
- Autoimmune diseases usually improved or occasionally were sent into remission
- Arthritis (mild, moderate, and even severe) usually improved or was managed, and for some completely cleared up
- Heartburn usually gone or improved
- Enlarged prostate usually improved or reduced to normal
- Gout usually cured, managed, or improved
- Gallstones usually cleared up or improved
- Erectile dysfunction (ED) usually improved or resolved
- Immune system strengthened
- Aging process slowed down
- Joint aches usually improved or eliminated
- Hormones usually balanced or improved
- Polycystic ovary syndrome usually improved or managed

One more thing I noticed with my patients: they had tremendous hope! That alone was worth every effort to push them closer toward a healthy lifestyle.

I knew what I needed to do.

OPEN IT UP TO THE REST OF THE WORLD!

Remember the woman with dementia? When she went on the ketogenic diet, her cholesterol dropped. She no longer needed her cholesterol-lowering medications. (I have said for years that those drugs have negative side effects, principally with brain function.) She was, admittedly, in a very tough situation. Thankfully, the diet worked, and she was able to regain her mental clarity and overcome dementia. The weight she lost as a result of the ketogenic diet was not only an added bonus, it was an integral part of her success.

I was hesitant to recommend the diet to other patients as a weight-loss program. I knew without a doubt that the diet would usually improve virtually everything that ailed them, but the words of my instructor still rang in my ears that no one could stick to a ketogenic diet.

Why the hesitancy to recommend this diet beyond just my patients who were sick or dying?

Quite simply, everyone is so scared about fats and cholesterol and heart disease, I did not want to be sued for recommending a diet that caused someone to have a heart attack. I did not think the diet would do that. In fact, I believed the exact opposite. But if someone believes fat will kill them and they get on this diet and die, no doubt they would blame me. At least that was my thinking.

But after tweaking and refining the ketogenic diet more and

more, and after seeing so many lives positively impacted and count-less diseases beaten, I decided it was time to take it to the world.

I know it works. It is balanced. And it is effective.

Now I present to you the Keto Zone diet, a combination of reduced carbs, increased healthy fats, and a moderate amount of healthy proteins.

"I lost 89 pounds in 14 months.
I feel happy, healthy, and alive.
I think everyone can do it."
—*Lacey*

CHAPTER TWO

LOOKING BACK AT HISTORY

IN THE MID-1800S, an English undertaker by the name of William Banting was trying in vain to lose weight. He only gained more. Medical doctors told him what most doctors tell their patients today: restrict calories and exercise more. This did not work. He had also tried laxatives, diuretics, Turkish baths, and starvation diets, among his twenty failed attempts at losing weight.

Banting also suffered from a painful umbilical hernia that required constant bandaging, and his knees ached so badly that he wrapped them to get some relief. Climbing stairs was difficult, and doing so left him short of breath and perspiring heavily. He was short and weighed more than two hundred pounds. Banting was desperate for answers.

One day he made an appointment with Dr. William Harvey for a hearing problem. Harvey had studied in Paris and recommended a new diet for Banting that included meat, fish, and poultry, along with no limit on animal and dairy fat. It also included small amounts of fruits that were low in sugar and only a few bites of toast. No other sweets, sugars, or starches were allowed.

It was a low-carb, high-fat diet of sorts, and it worked. Banting lost about fifty pounds in a year, suffering no side effects as he had with previous diets. In addition, this diet gave him more energy, lessened his knee pain, and reduced the gasping and profuse sweating he suffered after climbing stairs.

Banting was so excited about his weight loss that he wrote a small book about his story and the diet that changed his life. Demand for his book was great, and it was published and translated into many languages. Banting's popularity grew so much that the question "Do you Bant?" was synonymous with "Do you diet?" When people thought of dieting, they thought of Banting.

LEARNING FROM HISTORY

Banting was not the first to understand the benefits of a low-carb, high-fat diet. It turns out that this knowledge informed the daily lives of generations of Eskimo and Inuit in the Arctic.

In 1906 Vilhjalmur Stefansson, a Harvard-trained anthropologist and genuine risk taker, went on an adventure of a lifetime. He lived in the Canadian Arctic with the Inuit and ate only what they ate for an entire year. Approximately 75 percent of their calories came from fat. Interestingly, the lean pieces of meat were fed to the dogs. Vegetables were for times of famine.

By our standards, the Inuit were inexplicably healthy. They were not obese or disease-ridden. There was no scurvy from the expected lack of vitamin C. There were simply no health problems at all.

The answer was in the meats and fats and animal parts (such as bone marrow) that they ate. They had a use for practically every piece of the animal. All the necessary nutrients were there, and the Inuit were healthy as a result.

In 1928 Stefansson and a colleague checked into a hospital in New York City, publicly vowing to eat only meat and drink only water for a year. Pandemonium and protests erupted in the medical community, but after three weeks of the regimen, they were allowed to go home and continue the experiment from there. They ate the entire animal, including the meat, fat, brain, bones, and organs they knew contained the vitamins they needed. A barrage of tests a year later indicated that they were perfectly healthy—no deficiencies, no high blood pressure, no scurvy, no hair loss, no negative side effects at all.

Around that time several medical institutions (such as Johns Hopkins, Cornell University, and the Mayo Clinic) were using a similar diet high in fat and low in carbohydrates to treat children with seizures. The results were incredible, and many patients became seizure-free. For several decades, using a ketogenic diet to help treat seizures, especially in children, was an effective method.

When additional seizure-combating medications were brought to market in the early 1940s, the ketogenic diet became less and less popular and virtually disappeared. Medication all but replaced the it. (Incidentally, the ketogenic diet is still used in a few medical institutions to help treat, and many times cure, seizures in children.)

The advancement of medicine curtailed the growth of the ketogenic diet, but it was the branding of fat as the "greatest killer of our age" that really brought an end to the diet being a viable option for anything.

FAT IS BRANDED A KILLER

In the 1950s Ancel Keys, a biologist and pathologist at the University of Minnesota, believed there was a direct correlation between fat intake and heart disease. He pursued this belief with reckless abandon, launching two separate studies of multiple European countries that he felt proved his theory to be true.

In both studies, he chose countries that fit his criteria. Despite conflicting data, unequal measurements, the hiding of certain research, and flat-out inconsistencies, Keys used these studies and his charisma to tout the message that fat was bad, a diet high in fat caused heart disease, and anyone who disagreed with his findings was a quack. Eventually he concluded that saturated fat was the main enemy causing heart disease. After all, high cholesterol increases the risk of heart disease and saturated fats increased the cholesterol.

Every medical association and food-related government agency went along with his reports. Fat was branded a killer. The suggested daily intake of fats was slashed, and the low-fat, high-carb diet was not only recommended, it was now "proven" to be healthy.

Naturally, processed foods needed to contain less fat than ever before. Other industries needed to come up with low-fat, skim, lite, or lean versions of the normal. New oils and butter spreads were manufactured. To some extent, it did not matter what it was or what the side effects might be; as long as it was low-fat, it was deemed "healthy."

IT'S A FACT

Heart disease rates did not go down by avoiding saturated fats.

Along the way various scientists, researchers, and doctors stepped forward with their own vastly different conclusions. Keys was a master at destroying the credibility of anyone who questioned his findings, and few escaped unscathed. Stefansson, the explorer who had spent a year with the Inuit and had proven through his year long meat and water diet that the ketogenic diet was indeed healthy and did not cause heart disease, was dismissed by Keys as a quack. Stefansson's work was deemed irrelevant, and when he died in 1962, the ketogenic diet as a whole seemed to die with him.

With virtually everyone (the government, medical associations, education system, media, food companies, pharmaceutical companies, and doctors) participating, nations that adopted the fat-is-bad mentality should at the very least be able to boast incredibly low rates of heart disease. After all, more than fifty years of doing the right thing should have brought about the right results.

Sadly, that is not the case.

Why not? In a nutshell, Keys was wrong, the world believed him, and everyone has paid the price for it.

Every doctor would agree that if you were to compare our health today with the average health of people fifty years ago, you would find these diseases skyrocketing:

- Heart disease
- Type 2 diabetes
- Obesity
- Dementia
- Alzheimer's disease
- High blood pressure
- Children with pre-diabetes or type 2 diabetes
- ADD and ADHD
- Metabolic syndrome
- Preventable diseases

Over the years various studies disproved the supposed direct correlation between saturated fats and heart disease. Many of the researchers were mocked, but posthumously they have been proven right.

Very interestingly, in 1999 the Italian researcher Alessandro Menotti, who was the lead researcher of Keys's famous Seven-Countries Study, reanalyzed the data. He found that it was sweets, not fats, that had a greater influence on heart disease.[3]

Today Keys, known as the "father of cholesterol," would probably not have gotten away with such shoddy research. As one recent researcher noted, "To simply pick out the statistics that fit one's theory is a fatal scientific sin."[4] Keys is also credited as being the "father of the lipid hypothesis," which is a theory that there is a link between cholesterol levels and the risk of heart disease. The cholesterol controversy relates intake of saturated fats to heart disease.

The world believed Keys. But our findings today paint a very different picture. "We now know from the research that sugars and refined carbs are the true cause of obesity and heart disease—not fats, as we've been told," wrote Mark Hyman, medical director of the UltraWellness Center and Cleveland Clinic's Center for Functional Medicine. "Carbs turn on the metabolic switch, causing a spike in the hormone insulin, and this leads to fat storage (especially dangerous belly fat)."[5]

Despite researchers from all around the world stepping forward with proof that Keys was wrong, it was too late. Virtually the entire world bought into the belief that fat was bad.

However, facts and honest research have a way of being persistent. It is this stubborn refusal by some doctors, researchers, nutritionists, and even patients that is helping bring about a paradigm shift. Certain fats are very healthy, and other fats are very inflammatory. The right fats are critical for good health.

The paradigm shift is taking an incredibly long time to happen because so many people, businesses, and agencies believed Keys and because so much money was spent on his research.

Thankfully the shift back toward a more balanced diet is happening nonetheless.

THE RETURN OF THE KETOGENIC DIET

One of the medical doctors who spoke the loudest in favor of the ketogenic diet and its high-fat consumption, which flew directly in the face of society and all things medical, was Robert Atkins. He opened his cardiology practice in New York City in the 1960s. He was young, yet he was overweight, lethargic, and frustrated at his inability to tame his body.

In looking for answers, he discovered a low-carbohydrate diet by Dr. Alfred Pennington. Following that diet, Atkins lost weight easily. He was even hired by a company to help its employees lose weight, and he was incredibly successful at doing so.

Over the years, Atkins refined his diet to be a low-carb, high-fat, high-protein diet. As his reputation spread, his diet eventually ended up in *Vogue* magazine and was called the "Vogue diet" for a while. In 1972, he finally published *Dr. Atkins' Diet Revolution*, a book that sold tens of millions of copies and would become the best-selling diet book of all time.

> ### IT'S A FACT
>
> Trans fats, banned for being bad for our health, are often replaced with interesterified (IE) fats, which are worse. In IE fats, the fatty acids are moved from one triglyceride molecule to another in order to change the melting point and keep the oil from becoming rancid as quickly.

As expected, controversy swirled around Atkins, who was labeled a "quack," and his high-fat diet. He was ridiculed, mocked, and maligned and almost had his medical license revoked. Part of the resistance was based on the fact that Atkins did not have extensive studies proving his efforts. He did have countless testimonies or positive examples of how it worked, including real numbers from real people, but to the medical community, an official study meant more than best-selling books and thousands of testimonies.

Harvard's Frederick Stare, a nutritionist who is considered one of the most influential teachers in the country, testified before the Senate Select Committee on Nutrition and Human Needs in April 1973 about Atkins. "Any book that recommends unlimited amounts of meat, butter, and eggs . . . is dangerous," he said. "The author who makes the suggestion is guilty of malpractice."

I had a chance to talk with Atkins quite a few times in the 1990s and early 2000s at medical conferences. We discussed health and diets, and I peppered him with questions about the newest advances in nutritional medicine. In 2003, Atkins slipped and fell on an icy sidewalk, fracturing his skull. He died nine days later.

Keys died in 2004, a year after Atkins. During the fifty years of research and study by Keys, rates of heart disease increased, despite concerted global efforts to trim the fat from our diets. In truth, we are worse off now than when Keys started.

New research and numerous studies are showing that Atkins, and many others who are speaking up against the low-fat, high-carb craze, were and are right on target. Researchers Jeff Volek and Stephen Phinney, both from the fitness side of things, ran studies to verify their beliefs. Their findings revealed, among countless other things, the following about the Atkins diet:

- The low-carb diet works.
- Cardiovascular health is not impaired.

- The high-fat part of the diet actually lowers risk for heart disease and diabetes.
- HDL (the good cholesterol) goes up.
- Triglycerides, blood pressure, and inflammation go down.[6]

As for Keys's theory that fat, and especially saturated fat, was the cause of heart disease, that has been firmly debunked. Rajiv Chowdhury and his team reviewed seventy-two of the best studies on fat and heart disease that included more than six hundred thousand people from eighteen countries. They conclusively found there to be no evidence of a connection between dietary fat or saturated fat and heart disease.[7]

There is no going back and undoing history. The belief that fat is bad is still cemented as a "proven fact" in the minds of many, but that ship, though it has sailed, is leaking like a sieve.

Yes, fat (especially saturated fat) is still regarded as the enemy. Ask a doctor and you will probably get the same warning about not eating too many eggs, too much animal protein, avoiding butter, eating more fruit and vegetables, taking a statin drug to lower cholesterol, and more. And to lose weight, most doctors still recommend a low-fat diet.

Eventually, whether out of a desire to lose weight or out of desperation to beat a sickness, people are going to come face to face with the benefits of a ketogenic diet. At that point, they will have to make up their minds and choose what they are going to believe.

> **IT'S A FACT**
>
> There is zero correlation between the intake of saturated fat and heart disease.

A REVISED AND UPGRADED KETOGENIC DIET

In more than thirty years of medical practice, I have dissected almost every diet that exists. I have measured, counted, and calculated and have learned what does and does not work for weight loss. I have monitored, advised, and worked directly with thousands of patients to help them get healthy and stay healthy.

Though Atkins was right on target with many aspects of his diet, I am proposing a ketogenic diet that is different from his for two primary reasons:

1. *Protein:* Eating too much protein causes the body to convert excess proteins to sugar, which defeats part of the benefits of the ketogenic diet. Choose grass-fed meats and wild fish instead of processed meats, grain-fed meats, or farm-raised fish. There are too many toxins in these.
2. *Healthier fats:* Eating just any fat may work for weight loss on the ketogenic diet, but over the long term, it is much better to eat healthy fats, as they are not inflammatory.

I believe the Keto Zone diet is the healthiest diet in the world. The diet, in my opinion, is more important than any medicine, exercise, or supplements. The food that is the diet is what makes it work. Nothing else compares for weight loss, for overcoming or managing sicknesses and disease, and for creating a healthy and balanced lifestyle going forward.

If you have loved ones who have struggled with weight loss or who may have cancer, type 2 diabetes, Alzheimer's, Parkinson's, autoimmune disorder, obesity, heart disease, or another ailment, you may now have a very real answer for them.

As you know, I cannot say the Keto Zone diet will cure *every* disease. I could get sued for that. But I will boldly state that the Keto Zone diet will go a long way in helping treat, manage, reverse, and sometimes cure many diseases.

And if you are looking to lose weight, the Keto Zone diet is ideal. It works incredibly well. And the positive side effects are off the charts.

What are you waiting for?

"I lost 98 pounds in 15 months. I used to be tired, lethargic, cranky, and depressed. Everything has changed!"
—*Dan*

CHAPTER THREE
RISE OF THE NEW EPIDEMICS

LOUISE SAID SHE WANTED TO LOSE twenty pounds. I explained how the Keto Zone diet worked, helped her get the diet going, and gave her a few recipes, and then she took the plan and ran with it.

A few months later, she was back. The twenty pounds were gone. "I have a lot more energy, my mind is sharper, and I lost weight!" she beamed. "This is the best weight-loss program ever."

I smiled. If Louise can do it and succeed at age seventy, then the rest of us have no real excuse.

Not long after, a husband and wife came to the office. They were in their late forties. Though not obese by definition, they were clearly heading in that direction. Unless they chose to do something different, it was only a matter of time.

The husband explained, "We don't eat a lot of desserts. We go for walks, eat lots of fruits and vegetables, eat only whole-wheat bread, and always try to avoid fats. We are following our doctor's orders and eating healthy, but it's not working."

The wife added, "I have tried numerous diets myself, but I found the weight always seemed to come back, and then some."

I told them about Louise losing twenty pounds so effortlessly at her age. That seemed to motivate them.

Then I explained how the average person, if eating the low-fat, high-carb diet as instructed by every medical, food, nutrition, and government agency, will most likely continue to gain more and more weight.

"What makes this worse is that this process of weight gain speeds up as we age," I explained. "It really kicks in around age fifty."

They looked at each other and said at the same time, "What do we need to do?"

THE RIPPLE EFFECT

People come to my office all the time looking for help shedding those stubborn pounds or begging for help to stop the ever-increasing weight gain. Their weight is uncontrollable.

How is it that we, with all our technological advances and medical breakthroughs and limitless educational opportunities, have such bad food habits that we eat ourselves sick? Don't we know any better?

Apparently not. In 1960, only one in seven Americans was obese. Today we are at one in three, and by the year 2050, estimates are that the ratio will be one in two.[8]

When the "father of cholesterol" Ancel Keys started the low-fat, high-carb revolution, it became the gold standard for health and nutrition. It also started the biggest multi-trillion-dollar ripple effect of all time.

IT'S A FACT

Sodas and other sugary beverages spike the blood sugar and insulin levels and lead to weight gain.[9]

Ripple effect: The medical community followed
Keys's faulty findings.

With the American Medical Association and the American Heart Association recommending lower fat and higher carb intake, what could the food companies do except go with the flow?

Ripple effect: The food companies followed
the medical advice.

Processed foods became more and more the standard within society; from the grains in fresh bread to food that comes in boxes and from dairy to canned vegetables, everything changed.

Ripple effect: The foods became less nutritious
than ever before.

Out went the "bad" natural fats, only to be replaced with highly processed starches, high fructose corn syrup, artificial sweeteners, and preservatives.

Ripple effect: Everyone ate more carbs, as instructed.

In addition to eating low-fat, it was recommended that most of our daily calories come from carbohydrates. What could go wrong?

Ripple effect: Eating the recommended daily allowance
of carbs produced weight gain in children and adults,
and disease followed right behind.

It was at this point that man began to really fly. I am not talking about the Wright brothers and their first airplane. Rather, I am talking about the speed at which we ran toward disease.

The ripple effect from this point forward was exponential. There are approximately thirty-five major diseases that are directly connected to obesity rates. Usually, the more weight we gain, the sicker we get, and the numbers typically get worse.

So in essence, the obesity epidemic may be triggering the rise of approximately thirty-five other epidemics!

Speaking of numbers, it is estimated that by 2030 the US costs of all these preventable diseases will reach almost fifty trillion dollars cumulatively.[10]

Who is going to pay for all that?

As a medical doctor, the key word for me in all of this is *preventable*. In more than thirty years of practicing medicine and after treating thousands of patients for weight loss and disease, there is no question in my mind that the obesity epidemic ravaging our nation is completely and without question preventable.

But rather than going to the root of the problem, which is the food we are eating, our habit is to address the symptoms.

Ripple effect: We create more and more medicines,
pills, drugs, supplements, and surgeries to try to combat
the effects of our "healthy" low-fat, high-carb diet.

Disease rates are increasing at a mind-boggling speed, but we are not really doing anything to stem the tide. Coming up with a new drug is not helping much, nor is another low-fat yogurt or a new cholesterol-lowering margarine or slightly revised USDA guidelines or even new-and-improved school lunches.

In hindsight, it would have been better if we just ate the natural sugars, fats, and other ingredients that were in the food to begin with. But we cannot go back and redo the past.

Regardless of what we did right or wrong before, there is no question that we need to do things differently going forward. That is going to require that we not only see things differently but that we understand certain facts and act accordingly.

There are three foundational health truths that each one of us needs to understand in today's culture. Armed with that reality, we can navigate through life and achieve the results we want with greater ease.

We need to do things differently.

HEALTH TRUTH 1

See Sugar and Excessive Carbohydrates as the Enemy

In 1999, when Italian researcher Alessandro Menotti reanalyzed the data from the infamous Keys's Seven-Countries Study, he found that sweets had a greater influence on heart disease than fats.

Sweets? Really? Could the real cause of the obesity epidemic be the sweets we eat in the form of sugars, carbs, starches, and high fructose corn syrup?

> **IT'S A FACT**
>
> If life is a tragedy, sugar is the true villain.

Recognize that we are not just talking about table sugar or candy. The excess carbohydrates and starches we eat are eventually broken down to sugar. Carbs also come in the forms of fruits, bread, certain vegetables (especially potatoes), pasta, beverages, sauces, condiments, most dairy products, canned goods, desserts, yogurt, cereals, grains (wheat, corn, rice, oats), juices, and much more.

Yes, exactly; sugar is in virtually everything we eat.

Carbohydrates in the form of wheat, corn, rice, and potatoes are the most consumed sources of carbs. Our bodies convert these carbs and starches to sugar, which spikes insulin levels, and then usually store any extra calories as fat.

Those carbohydrates in the form of breads, gluten-free cereals, tortillas, rice, pasta, and potatoes are doing us all in. Consider this from cardiologist William Davis: "Aside from some extra fiber, eating two slices of whole wheat bread is really little different, and often worse, than drinking a can of sugar-sweetened soda or eating a sugary candy bar."[11]

We will talk more about carbs converting to sugar later. For now, know that sweets invite disease in and are the enemy of weight loss. Though sugar may not be your friend, it is nonetheless everywhere.

The low-fat, high-carb revolution that started in the 1950s brought with it the explosive growth of preventable diseases. What is the fuel behind every one of these diseases? Yes, you guessed it: sugar and excessive carbohydrates and starches.

IT'S A FACT

White rice is more potent than sweet soda drinks in causing diabetes, and a plate of white rice a day on a regular basis increases the risk of diabetes by 10 percent.[12]

Maybe you are thinking, *But I don't eat that much sugar or carbohydrates in a day.* But you may be surprised to find what is happening at the national level. Studies show that Americans on average eat 19.5 teaspoons (82 grams) of sugar every single day.[13] To look at this crazy statistic in weight, that is close to 66 pounds of sugar in a year per person.[14] Some say the number is much higher, with estimates of

152 pounds of sugar and 146 pounds of flour consumed by the average American each year.[15]

This amount of sugar consumed on a daily basis is not an issue that can be resolved by brushing our teeth more. Once the sugar (in its various forms, such as breads, pasta, juice, and cereal) gets into our bodies, it creates a chain of events that causes untold damage.

If that is not enough, the sugar itself is not to be taken lightly:

- Sugar is addictive, as much or more than cocaine or alcohol.[16]
- Sugar makes you hungry and want to eat more.[17]
- Sugar interferes with your appetite hormones, which means your body cannot tell when it is truly hungry or full. As a result, you eat more.[18]

In addition, as it relates to food, I have found that:

- Sugar raises insulin, programming you for more fat storage.
- Sugar usually gives you a "downer" feeling later, which leads to irritability, lethargy, depressed feelings, and more sugar intake to bring you out of that state.
- Sugar prevents you from burning fat when you work out at the gym.

To make matters even worse, many years ago someone had the bright idea of manufacturing artificial sweeteners. What could go wrong? Maybe it was a cost-saving measure or maybe it was an effort to decrease calories—it does not really matter. What matters is what happens to your body when you ingest them. Here is a snapshot:

- Increased appetite
- Insatiable food cravings
- Weight gain
- Appetite hormones imbalance
- Direct links to obesity and diabetes
- Good gut bacteria damaged

Some artificial sweeteners are more like a pesticide than a sugar. And similar to pesticides, some of the chemicals are stored in your body as toxins because they cannot be broken down. Trust me, you do not want your body storing toxins, and that is precisely what typically happens when you use artificial sweeteners.

> ### IT'S A FACT
>
> With natural sweeteners, such as stevia or monk fruit, liquid products are a bit better than powder because powders have tiny amounts of maltodextrin, an additive with caloric content. There are no calories in the liquid version.

When it comes to weight loss, sugars and artificial sweeteners will knock you out of the Keto Zone, which is the state at which optimal fat burning takes place. We will discuss this further in the pages to come, but for the sake of weight loss alone, you need to almost completely avoid sugars and artificial sweeteners in all forms.

Sadly, sugar is in virtually everything we eat. On top of that, it is the fuel behind many preventable diseases that are killing millions of people every single year. Pretty scary, isn't it?

If you are wondering if we are doomed to a life of bland food, know that we are not.

Or maybe we are doomed to a life of sickness? No to that as well.

As for sugars and sweeteners for beverages and cooking, there are several forms of natural sweeteners that are safe. I recommend stevia, monk fruit, and sweet alcohols such as erythritol and xylitol. These are healthy and have a low calorie count, which make them ideal for healthy living and weight loss in the Keto Zone diet. Stevia and monk fruit are both in powder or liquid forms, though liquid is a bit better. (Be careful not to use excessive amounts of xylitol since it can cause gastrointestinal disturbances.)

What about regular sugar, candy, syrup, honey, juices, cookies, breads, pasta, pies, cakes, and all the other countless forms of "sweets" that we grew up on and do not want to leave behind? The answer is to avoid them for now and start making healthy desserts that help push you toward your weight-loss goals.

HEALTH TRUTH 2

Know That All Fat Is NOT Your Enemy

I used to think that saturated fat was bad. Come on, everybody has been taught that, right? But is it true? Consider this:

Once you understand and start eating healthy fats, you will control appetite, tame hunger, lose weight, eliminate inflammation, and find your body will usually start to heal itself.

That is a proven fact. And that is healthy. It is also a bit of a mental jump!

To start with, know that we are talking about choosing the right combination of fish oil, healthy monounsaturated fats, and healthy saturated fats; minimizing polyunsaturated fats and choosing healthy ones (for example, walnuts and cold-pressed oil such as grape-seed oil); and never cooking with polyunsaturated fats.

Here are a few more facts that might surprise you about fats not being bad for your heart:

- The greater the intake of saturated fats, the less plaque buildup in the arteries.[19]
- Replacing carbs with protein or fat lowers blood triglyceride levels and increases HDL levels.[20]
- Eating saturated fats decreases the small dense atherogenic LDL and increases the nonharmful big, puffy LDL.[21]
- More than seventy academic studies have found the consumption of saturated fat, despite what we have been taught for generations, is not the cause of heart disease.[22]

Admittedly, it may take awhile for the new reality—that certain fats are indeed good for you—to sink in and even longer for that reality to become a natural part of life.

Yes, it goes against much of what we have been taught, but it is impossible to argue that our current recommended low-fat, high-carb diet we have followed for generations is actually making us healthier. Quite the opposite is true!

How does eating healthy fats play a part in the Keto Zone diet? And how does it help you lose weight? In a nutshell (and completely explained in the pages to come), this is what happens when your body is in the Keto Zone:

Your body burns stored excess fat as fuel when you reduce your carb intake enough. The healthy fats aid in the fat burning, increased metabolism, appetite control, reduced food cravings, increased energy, feelings of happiness, and clear thinking.

Eating a moderate amount of protein, along with the healthy fats and reduced carbohydrates, turns your body into a fat-burning machine. It is not only natural and healthy; it is really incredible to experience.

For now, know that fat is not your enemy.

HEALTH TRUTH 3

Accept the Rules Have Changed

The third foundational health truth is for many the biggest "ah-ha" moment in their understanding of what the Keto Zone diet is, because it helps them understand how it works. When they understand this, all the other pieces of the puzzle seem to fall into place. That is because the rules have changed.

To set the stage, consider this question you may have asked yourself: *Why can't I eat what I used to and get away with it?*

My patients ask me this all the time. They are shocked and genuinely angry that their bodies cannot keep up with the foods and drinks they are used to consuming. All was fine back when they were younger, so where did these muffin tops, love handles, potbellies, menopots, and more come from?

> ### IT'S A FACT
>
> When you control your insulin levels, you control your weight loss. A serum insulin level of 3 or lower is usually associated with weight loss.

What my patients have done is come face to face with the cold, hard, unyielding reality of carbohydrate sensitivity. This is their new norm, whether they like it or not.

Most people slowly build up a sensitivity to carbohydrates and become insulin resistant as they age, with the tipping point usually being around the age of fifty. If a man has a forty-inch waistline, he is already carbohydrate sensitive and insulin resistant (thirty-five inches for women).

This carbohydrate sensitivity and insulin resistance are what translate directly into belly fat.

Our bodies naturally produce insulin to lower, balance, and use the sugars we eat (unless we are type 1 diabetics). But as we age, things begin to change.

Insulin is a hormone. At the cellular level, it binds to receptors on the cell surface and then allows sugar to pass into the cell (similar to a key opening a lock, with insulin being the key and the receptor as the lock). This makes it possible for the sugar to be taken from the blood, transported into the cell, and used as energy. Basically, insulin is required to put the sugar to work.

However, if your body is carbohydrate sensitive and therefore insulin resistant, the receptors on the cell membrane act like a rusty lock. When insulin tries to bind to the receptors on the cell's surface, it cannot bind as well. As a result, some sugar is unable to enter the cell, and it stays in the blood. Then both sugar and insulin levels rise in the blood.

Rising sugar levels mean your body needs to produce even more insulin to try to get the sugar into the cells. Your pancreas will keep producing more and more insulin in an effort to lower your blood sugar. This in turn has further ramifications. In the area of weight loss, two very disappointing things occur.

First, your key appetite hormones that tell you when you are hungry or full become all scrambled up as a result of the excessive amounts of insulin.

When my patients complain that they can eat a huge meal and still feel hungry, it is precisely this scrambling of appetite hormones that is taking place. It is almost impossible to lose weight if they cannot manage their appetite, and they are unable at this point to manage their appetite because of the excessive insulin. They are stuck. (More on this subject in chapter 10.)

Second, insulin resistance literally blocks your body from burning fat.

For years my patients have been saying about the same thing: "It seems the more carbs I eat, the less my body can lose weight." They are absolutely right. They cannot burn fats because the excessive carb intake and elevated insulin levels are blocking the entire fat-burning process. High insulin is like flipping a switch that programs the body for fat storage, especially the dreaded belly fat. Get your serum insulin levels checked, and if they are over 3, then there's a very good chance you are having a difficult time losing weight.

It is at this point of prolonged insulin resistance that we begin to see metabolic syndrome, pre-diabetes, and eventually type 2 diabetes, and a host of other diseases begin to raise their ugly heads.

The great news is that carbohydrate sensitivity and insulin resistance can be broken down. For those seemingly stuck in a lose-lose battle with their weight, there is a way out. It is possible to get your body back on track, control your hormones, manage your appetite, and lose weight.

That is why lowering insulin levels, which is what happens in the Keto Zone diet, is so absolutely necessary. By lowering insulin levels, you enable your body to keep losing weight, as much as you want. When you control your insulin levels, you are the one in control.

With all that said, let me remind you what we are all told to eat on a daily basis. The 2015–2020 Dietary Guidelines for Americans said we should all consume 45 to 65 percent of our calories from carbohydrates.[23] You have just programmed yourself for fat storage!

Most people who eat the recommended daily allowances are going to gain weight, eventually become obese, and be forced to contend with the many preventable diseases that follow directly after obesity. What that means is that most of us, especially as we age, need to be on a lower carbohydrate diet than when we were younger. We need to accept that the rules have changed and do something about it.

You now know some of the effects, causes, and logic behind the foods we eat. Knowledge not only brings power, it also brings hope, and that is a very good thing when it comes to food, diets, family, fun, and a healthy lifestyle.

GETTING YOUR LIFE BACK

Thankfully, our bodies were made in such a way that we can go to the source (the food) and make changes that will have a cascading positive effect on every area of our lives. I have seen so many patients overcome their "impossible" situations and get their lives back (literally in some cases) that I have no doubt we can all overcome what ails us.

I follow that encouragement with strong advice to start right away, as we are all on a clock. And practically speaking, the sooner you start, the sooner you can get your life back to the way you want it.

How does all this play into the Keto Zone diet? It fits beautifully. Let me explain in brief:

Suppose your body can burn 100 grams of carbs per day and not gain any fat. Everyone is different, but let's say that is your ideal carb management number.

Now, if you are getting your USDA-recommended daily allowance of carbs, you are clocking in around 200 to 300 grams of carbs a day. That is where the excess weight and health issues are coming from.

On the Keto Zone diet, we lower your daily carb intake to around 20 grams per day, boost your healthy fat intake, and maintain a moderate protein intake. That causes your body to shift to burning fat rather than using the usual sugar as fuel. You have just shifted into the Keto Zone or your fat-burning zone! You are now burning fat as your main fuel and not sugar.

Your insulin numbers come completely under your control at this point, and you can lose as much weight as you want. Carb sensitivity is not an issue because you have temporarily lowered your carb intake below your body's carbohydrate threshold for weight gain, and insulin levels drop dramatically, programming you for weight loss.

When you have reached your ideal weight, you dial up the carbohydrates from 20 grams to around 50 to 100 grams, and you are set. Lean body, healthy, and no more weight gain.

That is how it works. That is the Keto Zone diet in a nutshell. It sounds so simple, and it really is.

"I never knew how sugar
and starchy foods sabotaged
my weight loss efforts, until now."
—*Carrie*

CHAPTER FOUR

OVERVIEW OF THE KETO ZONE DIET

SALLY CAME TO MY OFFICE not long ago, desperate for answers. She explained how she had gained more than a hundred pounds in two years, hired a personal trainer for a year, and then gained twenty-five more pounds. She also suffered from polycystic ovaries and had fibroids.

"What am I doing wrong?" she pleaded. "I work out an hour a day, five days a week, I've followed my trainer's low-fat diet, and all I'm doing is gaining more weight!"

I commended her for her amazing tenacity to exercise that much every day, to get a personal trainer, and to work that hard. "However," I explained, trying to let her down gently, "it is not working for you because it cannot work for you."

"What?" she immediately demanded. "Then what is the answer?"

I explained that her basis for health and nutrition was all wrong. She was eating low-carb, but not low enough, which was causing her metabolism to slow down. Her fats were too low and her protein intake was too high, which only added to more sugar production and more weight gain. To top it off, her workouts were burning glycogen (stored sugar) only, not fat, and once the stored sugar was depleted, she was hungrier for it. She complained of always being hungry.

She not only had the wrong game plan, she was playing the wrong game entirely. Based on what she was doing with her degree of carb sensitivity, it was almost impossible for her to lose weight.

> **IT'S A FACT**
>
> Ketosis is the natural, safe condition where your body is burning fat rather than sugar as its primary fuel source.

Now, *impossible* is not a word that people on a diet like to hear. Talk about a real killjoy! But the good news is that once she had the right game plan and started building on the right foundation, mixed with her incredible work ethic, the fat would burn right off. Hope came flooding back.

I explained the science behind the Keto Zone diet and how women with polycystic ovaries are especially carb sensitive and insulin resistant. Her eyes lit up as she came to understand the how-to-burn-fat paradox.

Taking immediate action, she gladly dove into the Keto Zone diet. We lowered her carbs to 20 grams per day, increased her healthy fat intake considerably, lowered her protein a bit, and added a few supplements that she was missing.

She immediately started losing weight.

At that point, with the fat melting away, she was angry with her personal trainer. "Why didn't he tell me?" she asked. She was frustrated that she had spent a year with nothing to show for it. I told her that it was not the trainer's fault. Trainers do their best to help people lose weight, but if they follow the same low-fat diet as the rest of society, the increased physical exercise is not necessarily going to work for weight loss.

As it turned out, Sally was her own before and after picture. The personal trainer contacted me and asked for more information. Now he puts all his clients on the Keto Zone diet.

THE BASICS OF THE KETO ZONE DIET

As we have discussed, the primary goal of the Keto Zone diet is to reduce your daily carbohydrate intake to below your body's carbohydrate threshold for weight gain. This in turn causes your body to burn excess fats rather than sugars as its fuel source.

The sugar your body usually burns is glucose, which is produced from the carbs (breads, sugar, pasta, potatoes, juices, sodas, fruits, and sugary beverages) you eat or drink. Any extra glucose is either stored in your liver or muscles as glycogen or converted to fat.

By lowering your carb intake, your insulin levels also drop and your metabolism eventually shifts into fat-burning mode. Eating foods that are healthy and speed up the fat-burning process (in the form of a high amount of healthy fats and a moderate amount of healthy protein) helps you control your appetite and reach your goal weight.

Those are the basic elements of the Keto Zone diet.

When your body is in this fat-burning mode, you are technically in the state of ketosis. Often misunderstood, the word *ketosis* is admittedly very scary sounding, which is one of the reasons why ketogenic diets as a whole have received such negative press. Scary! Bad! Dangerous! Unsafe! Deadly!

In truth, ketosis is the natural, safe condition where your body is burning fat rather than sugar as its primary fuel source.

You actually come close to ketosis when you sleep. If you eat dinner around 6 p.m. and drink only water before eating breakfast at 6 a.m., your body is very close to the ketosis state after twelve hours of fasting. Fasting longer than twelve hours does the same thing, even more so.

But after you eat breakfast or break your fast, your body usually does not return to ketosis again all day. That is because your body is busy digesting the food you have eaten and breaking down carbs and starches into sugar. If what you ate is the normal low-fat, high-carb diet, burning sugar is all that your body can do for the rest of the day.

> ## IT'S A FACT
>
> In the Keto Zone, your body is reprogrammed to burn fat. The first fat to go is usually belly fat.

Imagine instead if your body was burning fat all day long! Even better, imagine feeling full and satisfied, sharp and alert, with boundless energy and no food cravings for the entire day!

That is what typically happens to your body when you are in the Keto Zone.

KETO ZONE: WHAT YOU CAN EXPECT

Food is the focus, so it is only normal to wonder exactly what the expectations and limits are for the Keto Zone diet. From the perspective of carbs, fats, and protein, here is an approximate framework of what you will eat while in the Keto Zone:

Carbs: 10 to 15 percent of daily caloric intake from healthy carbs, such as salad veggies, nonstarchy vegetables, spices, and herbs.

Fats: 70 percent of daily caloric intake from healthy fats including omega-3 fats (fish oil), healthy monounsaturated fats, healthy saturated fats, and minimal healthy polyunsaturated fats.

Proteins: 10 to 15 percent of daily caloric intake from healthy protein, such as whole pastured eggs, wild low-mercury fish, and grass-fed meats, aiming for around 1 gram of protein per 1 kilogram of weight.[24]

When the daily recommended allowance for carbohydrates intake is reduced from 45 to 65 percent of total calories to 15 percent (some need a bit less than that), your body naturally begins to burn fat rather than sugar. Adding in moderate amounts of protein and high amounts of good fats, your body reaches its peak metabolic fat-burning zone.

What 10–15 percent of healthy carbs or proteins and 70 percent of healthy fats translate into as far as portions and meals and menus and real food, will be made plain in the pages to follow.

When you fuel your body with 10 to 15 percent healthy carbs, 70 percent healthy fats, and 10 to 15 percent healthy proteins, you are going to be in the peak metabolic fat-burning zone! It usually takes people one to three days to reach the Keto Zone (maybe seven to fourteen days for pre-diabetics and type 2 diabetics), but if it takes you longer than three days, rest assured you will get there. When in the Keto Zone, you can expect:

- Dangerous belly fat to usually burn off first
- Reduced appetite

- No food cravings, usually
- A loss of 4 to 5 pounds of fluid weight in the first week, then usually 1 to 2 pounds of fat per week after that (some lose 1 pound per day)
- After a month or more in the Keto Zone, many people are satisfied with only two meals a day, morning and early evening (usually after a month or more)
- Usually no hunger pangs
- Usually incredible energy, mental clarity, and focus
- No calorie counting required

WHAT HAPPENS TO YOUR BODY IN THE KETO ZONE

As you already know, once you have reached the Keto Zone, your body is burning fat rather than sugars. This is the ketosis process hard at work, brought on by the fact that you have lowered your carb intake considerably, down to around 20 grams per day to begin with, raising it up later after achieving your ideal weight.

When you are in ketosis, your body naturally produces acids in the blood called *ketones*, which are flushed out in the urine. These trace amounts of ketones are a sign that your body is breaking down fat.

For decades it has been known that eating a no-carb or low-carb diet (between 0 and 60 grams of carbs per day) with a moderate protein intake (around 1 gram of protein per 1 kilogram of weight) will produce ketones. That is a sign your body is in ketosis, which again is a natural and safe process. When you are burning fat rather than sugar because of your low-carb intake, your ketones usually measure at the very low 0.5 to 1 millimolar (mM) range. Blood pH levels are normal.

Start talking about ketosis and ketones and people usually say, "Wait a minute! I read about ketoacidosis, and it's dangerous."

They are right—ketoacidosis is dangerous, but it is also not the same as ketosis. Ketoacidosis is potentially fatal and is the result of very high blood ketone levels, which can occur in people with type 1 diabetes or rarely in type 2 diabetes who have destroyed most of their insulin-producing cells in the pancreas and require insulin. Unless you have type 1 diabetes or have advanced type 2 diabetes, you do not need to worry about ketoacidosis because it is impossible for your body to go there.

In nutritional ketosis, which is what we are talking about with the Keto Zone diet, you are in a healthy metabolic state where your blood sugar levels are normal and your ketones are low. In this state of nutritional ketosis, you are burning fat and controlling your hunger and appetite. Bring it on!

> ### IT'S A FACT
>
> Rest assured, when limiting carbohydrate intake to 20 grams per day, the vast majority of people will go into the Keto Zone and their bodies will begin burning fat rather than sugar.

The small amount of ketones in your urine simply shows that fat breakdown has been activated. That is all.

To further clarify, in a ketoacidosis state, blood pH levels are very low, blood sugar levels are extremely high, and people with type 1 diabetes and late-stage type 2 diabetes cannot produce insulin to counter the high blood sugars. Ketone levels are usually 15 to 25 millimolars, which is extremely high and thus incredibly dangerous. In nutritional ketosis, ketone levels are usually 0.5 to 5 millimolars, but more commonly 0.5 to 3 millimolars.

Clearly, ketosis and ketoacidosis are completely different. To many, however, they sound so similar that they are falsely assumed to be the same thing.

One more detail about your body in the Keto Zone that will interest you is the fact that spikes in insulin, which your body produces to lower your blood sugar, stop all production of ketones. Stop it completely! Eating sugary foods, starches, and carbs will usually spike sugar and insulin levels, but sodas, juices, sweetened coffees, sweet tea, smoothies, and many other beverages high in sugar will usually spike insulin levels more than eating sugary foods.

If your body cannot produce ketones, it is not burning fat, and if it is not burning fat, then you usually are not losing weight. That is another reason why lowering your insulin levels is absolutely essential in keeping your body in a peak fat-burning state.

Now, if you happen to have type 1 diabetes, I would recommend the anti-inflammatory foods outlined in my book *Let Food Be Your Medicine*. However, with your usual careful blood sugar management, using the Keto Zone diet is a healthy and viable option for you as well as long as you follow up with your physician regularly and adjust your insulin doses under your physician's guidance.

If you have advanced type 2 diabetes, ease into the Keto Zone diet. It will take longer to reach the desired Keto Zone, but you will eventually get there. I have seen this to be incredibly helpful for people with type 2 diabetes. Be careful, but the benefits, such as lowering your insulin dosages, are amazing. Monitor your blood sugar levels daily, and follow up with your physician regularly.

WAYS TO STAY IN THE KETO ZONE

Produced as a result of your body burning fats, ketones are the perfect measuring guide, like a car's dipstick if you will, to help keep you in the zone. In time and with practice, you will know when you are in the zone, but measuring your ketones is the fastest and easiest way to know you are right on track.

It usually takes a few days for your body to get into the Keto Zone, and with the small amounts of ketones in your urine, the initial and easiest way to measure is with a urine test strip. These ketone strips, such as Ketostix, are inexpensive and readily available at a local pharmacy or health food store. (You can even cut the strips in half to save a few dollars.) See appendix A for a source.

To see if you are in ketosis, pass the ketone strip through your urine stream, then wait fifteen seconds and compare the stick to the color chart on the side of the bottle.

Remember, it may take a few days to two weeks (for some people) for the small amount of ketones to register, but when ketones do register, then you know you are without question in ketosis, the fat-burning Keto Zone. You will be able to see, as you check two or three times a day, how your body is performing. Trust me, it is a very motivating feeling when you know your body is hard at work burning off unwanted fat.

> ### IT'S A FACT
>
> Your liver produces three different types of ketones: beta-hydroxybutyrate, aceto-acetate, and acetone. On a low-carb diet, these ketones increase in number.

After a month of burning fat in the Keto Zone, your body will be more adapted or used to being in ketosis. At that point, the ketones you have been measuring in your urine will eventually fade away.

What happened? How will you measure ketones?

What took place is that your body is adjusting even further into fat-burning mode. In the first month or so, your body produced a specific ketone, acetoacetate. That is the type of ketone the urine strips measure. As your body adjusts to your new fat-burning reality, it produces mainly two other ketones instead—acetone and beta-hydroxybutyrate.

The way to measure acetone and beta-hydroxybutyrate is with a ketone breath analyzer (to measure acetone) or a blood ketone monitor (to measure beta-hydroxybutyrate). These two other ketones will show up on the tests if you are still in the Keto Zone.

For best results, and until you feel you are consistently staying in the Keto Zone, the blood monitor or the breath analyzer is a good way to know precisely where you are. I recommend them, and both are available online. They are not as inexpensive as the strips, but either is very helpful. I prefer the Ketonix breath ketone analyzer (powered by a computer via its USB port).

As you watch the results of your efforts, you will know what it feels like to be solidly in the Keto Zone. If you are burning fat, not hungry, and sticking to your plan, then you are most likely right where you want to be—in the Keto Zone.

KETO ZONE: INCREDIBLY HEALTHY

The Keto Zone diet is the fastest and healthiest way to burn fat, especially belly fat, which is directly related to so many diseases. It also helps prevent, manage, and even cure countless sicknesses and diseases. As a reminder, ketogenic diets have been used to treat many conditions: infantile spasms, epilepsy, autism, brain tumors, Alzheimer's disease, Lou Gehrig's disease, depression, stroke, head trauma, Parkinson's disease, migraines, sleep disorders, schizophrenia, anxiety, ADHD, irritability, polycystic ovarian disease, irritable bowel syndrome, gastroesophageal reflux, obesity, cardiovascular disease, acne, type 2 diabetes, tremors, respiratory failure, and virtually every neurological problem, but also cancer and conditions where tissues need to recover after a loss of oxygen.[25]

Truly, being in the Keto Zone is more than just a great way to lose weight. It is an incredibly healthy way to live. If you happen to have any of the conditions listed above, the Keto Zone diet may be the answer.

For many years I have put cancer patients on a ketogenic diet with amazing results. By removing the sugar and starchy foods that cancer feeds on, the cancer loses its main fuel source, and many patients improve. I've done that for years, and research supports it.[26]

Though our society is well trained to think low-fat everything, your heart, brain, and kidneys work better when the source of fuel is fat rather than the usual glucose (sugar). In fact, your heart and brain run at least 25 percent more efficiently on fat than blood sugar.[27]

I have come to see that adding fat to our diet, such as olive oil, avocados, fish oil, almonds, pecans, macadamia nuts, and some healthy saturated fats such as medium-chain triglycerides (MCT) oil,

IT'S A FACT

Cut your carb intake, and your blood sugar and insulin levels naturally decrease.

grass-fed butter, and cocoa (dark chocolate), in my opinion actually reduces heart disease more than cholesterol-lowering statin drugs can. I recognize that is a pretty bold statement, but the results speak for themselves. So far more than seventy studies verify the fact that saturated fat is not the cause of heart disease.[28]

On the cellular level, the body produces the energy we need from the food we eat. If the source is sugar, the body produces insulin to lower the blood sugar levels, and excess sugar is stored either as glycogen or as fat. Due to our usual high-carb diet, much of the sugar is stored as fat, and until we enter the Keto Zone, the body will usually continue to burn sugar and store fat until we lower the carb level low enough to get the fat-burning engines going again.

If the source of energy is fat, rather than sugar, far greater energy is produced. In addition to fat being the best energy source, we also have more of it. That is because our bodies usually have more than 40,000 calories in fat stored away in our adipose tissue, but less than 2,000 calories in carbohydrates in storage.[29]

What that means is we usually don't need to worry about running out of energy on the ketogenic program. We virtually have no end to the reserves. And that is precisely why many weight lifters and athletes have used ketogenic diets to their advantage for decades.

What is more, and thankfully so, the Keto Zone diet works long term. It is a diet and lifestyle you can enjoy for years and years to come (more about that later). To me, it means I will not only be lean and healthy now, but I will be around to play with my grandchildren and even their children.

My best advice to you is to get in the Keto Zone and stay there so you can enjoy life and live it to its fullest.

"Having been a skeptic
about these types of programs,
I was hesitant about participating . . .
but I lost 12+ pounds in 21 days!"
—*Larry*

CHAPTER FIVE

BENEFITS OF BEING IN THE KETO ZONE

MY WIFE, MARY, is my greatest fan as well as my toughest critic. She is always honest and tells it like it is. I knew if she could do the Keto Zone diet, then anyone could.

Within six weeks, she had lost about twenty pounds, and after four months she had lost another thirty-five pounds.

"I had no hunger cravings, no sugar or carb cravings, and no light-headedness. Quite honestly, it was far easier than I expected," she said.

Like most people, Mary lost four to five pounds the first week, most of which was water that the body naturally stores. After the first week, she lost one to two pounds of fat a week. We added in some exercise (brisk walking, thirty minutes a day, five days a week) to her routine, and she increased the fat-burning rate to two to three pounds a week.

Even if you only lost a single pound per week, in a year that would be fifty-two pounds. Nobody would object to that! What is more, that type of gradual weight loss shows the person is on track and staying in the Keto Zone, which is peak fat-burning mode.

Typically, the simple act of walking fifteen to thirty minutes a day will turn up the burn to about two pounds of weight loss per week.

"In addition to always being hungry, most people on a diet are not sure what they can and cannot eat, so I had Don tell me what to eat, how to shop, and how to do this in the real world," Mary explained.

We worked together to clear out our pantry of foods that would bump us out of the Keto Zone. All the processed foods in boxes were the first to go. We then bought the right ingredients and began to cook differently. Living in the Keto Zone was easier than she first expected.

Not long ago while we were traveling, she took pictures of food in restaurants that she could eat and still remain in the Keto Zone. It helped prove the point that if you want to stay in the zone, you can do it, even if you are eating out.

As for you, there are many questions you may have about foods:

What can I eat? . . . *that is coming soon.*
How do I shop? . . . *coming soon.*
What can I not eat? . . . *coming soon.*
Are there delicious meals and recipes to make? . . . *coming soon.*

The Keto Zone diet is a unique program. You lose weight without starving yourself to death. But that is not all. On the Keto Zone diet, you can expect the following, usually:

- Virtually no hunger cravings
- Full appetite control
- A loss of 1 to 3 pounds per week
- Feelings of happiness
- Significant weight loss
- Plenty of energy
- Improved memory
- No brain fog

No complaints there! Where do I sign up?

MULTIPLIED BENEFITS

Weight loss is the goal, but in my mind as a medical doctor I find I am always thinking about my patients and their overall health and wellness. Thankfully, the Keto Zone diet accomplishes that goal as well.

The benefits I have seen with my patients would be a list that goes on for pages. Suffice to say, from migraines to memory loss to ADHD to insulin numbers to high blood pressure to depression to pre-diabetes to IBS to fibromyalgia to type 2 diabetes to arthritis to cancer and much more—the results have been astounding. It seems hard to believe, but I have found that you can usually improve and sometimes reverse most diseases by following the Keto Zone diet.

If a woman wants to fit into a pair of jeans or wear a certain dress that has been hanging in the back of the closet, she can do that and enjoy all the other health benefits that come with the Keto Zone diet.

If a man wants to play ball with his kids or get rid of his love handles, he can do that and lower his cholesterol and treat a host of other ailments at the same time.

On a somber note, if you have a family history of colon cancer, breast cancer, or pancreatic cancer, the Keto Zone will usually help.

Is Parkinson's disease, autoimmune disease, arthritis, dementia, or Alzheimer's disease in the family? You may be able to slam the door shut on those conditions with the Keto Zone diet.

For me, a big "ah-ha" moment came when I realized that not only did the Keto Zone diet offer a way to burn off stubborn fat, it also was the best form of protection from diseases.

> **IT'S A FACT**
>
> Decreasing carb intake directly improves acne.

The Keto Zone diet provides you with the best brain food possible, most inflammatory triggers are turned off, and fat is burned off at a heightened pace. (I am thinking of possible drawbacks to this, but have not found any.)

Clearly, this is a win-win scenario.

WE ALL GET TO CHOOSE

With such a list of benefits, it would seem logical that everyone wanting to lose weight and everyone wanting to overcome one of these sicknesses or diseases would jump into the Keto Zone diet.

But we love our food. We like our traditions. We have habits. We do not really want to change. Whatever the reason, as valid as it might be, the decision to change is always yours.

Imagine for a minute an entire nation that can boast of having the world's lowest heart disease rates, lowest cancer rates, lowest type 2 diabetes rates, lowest obesity rates, lowest dementia and Alzheimer's disease rates, and so on. They would be the healthiest people on the planet. From their pocketbook to their employment and from their fun to their family, every area of life would be positively affected.

Take type 2 diabetes as an example. It is an epidemic that costs billions of dollars every year to treat. But in one study alone, more than 95 percent of the type 2 diabetes patients reduced or eliminated their medications within six months of going on a low-carb diet like the Keto Zone diet.[30] I know of no better way to treat or even reverse type 2 diabetes, and that is only one disease.

If such a healthy nation existed, other countries would send delegates to find the secret to their amazing health. Entire industries would be created to support this healthy lifestyle. Trillions of dollars would be saved in medical and insurance costs, millions of lives would be saved, and that would literally transform entire nations.

This is beyond big—this is earth-shatteringly huge! But it is and always will be a choice made at the personal level. You and I get to choose.

I find my choices are based on what I want. I know someone else may want something for me, but only when I want it am I truly motivated to go after it.

What is it that you want? As practical as it might be, if it is important to you, then it is also motivating.

- Is it to wear that gorgeous expensive dress again?
- Is it to hold your head high at work?
- Is it to get that clean bill of health from your doctor?
- Is it to get down on the floor and play with your grandchildren?
- Is it to run that marathon or 5K run you have always talked about?

Whatever it is that moves you, whatever it is that you so desperately want and desire, let that be the spark that fires you up to chase your dreams. The Keto Zone diet can help you get there. It can and it will. I have seen it so many times.

And what is more, every step toward your dreams has countless other good, amazing, long-lasting benefits.

PART TWO

Why the Keto Zone Diet Works

Why the Keto Zone diet works, why each piece of the puzzle goes together so well, and why the Keto Zone diet is, indeed, the best and healthiest way to lose weight.

CHAPTER SIX

THE KETO ZONE AND YOUR CHOLESTEROL

"IF YOU WERE MY PATIENT, I would put you on a statin drug right away," said the doctor. "You need to lower your cholesterol."

Then the doctor went on to explain how her own father had almost died from a heart attack at age fifty. "He ignored his cholesterol numbers," she warned. "You need to do something right away."

At age forty-six, Ryan had moderately high cholesterol that had not changed much in years. His triglycerides were also a little high, while his HDL cholesterol or good cholesterol was a little low, but not alarmingly so.

People with high LDL numbers and high triglyceride numbers usually have a degree of insulin resistance, may be pre-diabetes, or may have metabolic syndrome. But Ryan did not have metabolic syndrome or pre-diabetes yet, but yes, he needed to do something. The answer, however, was not taking a statin drug.

I told Ryan, "In three months, we should have your LDL cholesterol and triglycerides lowered and your HDL raised. What you need to do is cut down dramatically your intake of both sugars and carbs and balance your fats."

Three months later, it was a completely different ball game. All his tests had improved and normalized.

CHOLESTEROL-TREATING OPTIONS

When it comes to cholesterol, people can get into trouble if they do not understand what the numbers actually mean. Typically, there are four ways to deal with cholesterol numbers:

- Ignore them completely
- Try an herb or supplement or "miracle cure"
- Take doctor-prescribed drugs
- Change the diet

We all would agree that ignoring something, especially our cholesterol numbers, will never fix anything. We cannot get the results we want by ignoring the problem, but you would be surprised by how many patients I have seen over the years who have tried this method. Ignorance is not bliss. Trust me, this never ends well.

There are a lot of "testimonials and quack science" floating around, much of which probably ends up in your e-mail spam folder, that promise a certain drink or powder or herb or seed or supplement or nutrient or exercise will magically lower your cholesterol. Yes, there are some supplements or herbs that may help, such as citrus bergamot, soluble fiber, and plant sterols, but many do not help at all.

The option that is seen by many to be the most solid and scientific answer is to take a doctor-prescribed statin drug to lower cholesterol. Statins are one of the most-prescribed drugs in America. The negative side effects are worth it, so discussion closed.

But are statin drugs the only solution?

There is another option, one that has been scientifically proven to be effective. It requires more effort and self-control than any of the other choices, which is one of the reasons why it is seldom chosen, but it usually works incredibly well. In addition, there are usually no bad side effects and some positive side effects.

This option is to change your diet. It is exactly what the Keto Zone diet is all about, and it is incredibly effective at lowering the bad LDL pattern B cholesterol (see "What Are Your Real Cholesterol Numbers" later in this chapter), lowering triglyceride levels, raising good cholesterol, treating high blood pressure, and reducing the risk for heart disease.

TALKING CHOLESTEROL NUMBERS

When it comes to achieving ideal cholesterol numbers, most doctors, as I used to do for many years, will say something like:

- LDL levels should be below 100 (mg/dL)
- Triglyceride levels should be below 150 (mg/dL)
- HDL cholesterol should be above 40 (mg/dL)
- Total cholesterol should be below 200 (mg/dL)

For those who ask what the acronyms mean, we tell them:

- *LDL* (the bad cholesterol) is low-density lipoprotein that carries fat through the bloodstream. Cholesterol by itself is unable to be dissolved in the blood and must be transported by carriers called lipoproteins, which are made up of fat and protein.

- *HDL* (the good cholesterol) is high-density lipoprotein. It carries LDL cholesterol away from the arteries and back to the liver where it is disassembled and excreted from the body.

- *Triglycerides* are fatty acids. Their key role is for long-term fat storage for the purpose of generating energy. However, high amounts of triglycerides in the blood are associated with plaque formation in the arteries.

But what are you to do with that information? Doctors, dieticians, and nutritionists will usually tell you to:

- Take statin drugs to lower your LDL numbers
- Lower your intake of saturated fats
- Cut out all foods with cholesterol
- Get more fiber (which is usually a good thing)
- Make sure your carbs are 45 to 65 percent of your calories
- Manage your weight
- Get more physical exercise

There we have it. And that is about as deep as most people, as well as most doctors, ever go on the subject of cholesterol. That is usually all they know.

But when it comes to cholesterol, *your* cholesterol, it pays to know more.

Did you know that cholesterol in your body does not mean you have plaque buildup? Not at all!

Maybe you thought, *Cholesterol is bad for my health.* In truth, your liver makes cholesterol all the time. Your body needs it. The one organ that needs cholesterol the most is your brain.

Or maybe you have been taught: *Cholesterol causes plaque buildup in my arteries.*

This is one of the biggest errors in our thinking. It is at this point that people assume cholesterol, all cholesterol, is bad and must be minimized in an effort to avoid plaque buildup and heart disease.

That was the same logic Keys, the "father of cholesterol," followed with his low-fat revolution. Remember how he tried to prove that higher saturated fat intake caused heart disease, but decades later it was shown that sugar is the main villain and not saturated fat?

But the belief that a low-fat, high-carb diet is good and healthy continues to move forward, especially when it comes to lowering

> ### IT'S A FACT
> Your liver makes most of the cholesterol that you have in your bloodstream.

cholesterol. At first glance, it is "easy" to connect fats with cholesterol, plugging arteries, plaque buildup, and all sorts of plumbing analogies.

But the answer is not blaming or banning cholesterol. High cholesterol is not the main cause of plaque. The real culprit is inflammation and oxidized cholesterol.

WHAT IS OXIDIZED CHOLESTEROL?

Oxidation is like rust that forms on a piece of iron left outside in the rain. The oxidation process inside your body is like rust damage to your cells. It is this oxidized cholesterol and inflammation that is mainly responsible for plaque buildup in your arteries. This naturally leads to the question: *What causes cholesterol to oxidize?*

Understand that your LDL cholesterol is most damaging to your arteries and most likely to cause plaque if it is oxidized by free radicals. Excessive dietary intake of unhealthy polyunsaturated fats (PUFAs), such as soybean oil (the most consumed oil in America), corn oil, sunflower oil, safflower oil, and canola oil, causes increased oxidation of LDL cholesterol, a process in which the LDL rancidifies or is damaged to the extent that it is very prone to form plaque in the arteries. When any polyunsaturated oil, including grape-seed oil, is exposed to heat, the LDL cholesterol becomes damaged by free radicals or is oxidized. For this reason, never cook with PUFA oils. Most restaurants, especially fast food restaurants, use these cheap inflammatory oils in most of their food.

There are healthy polyunsaturated fats (PUFAs) with a healthy ratio of omega-6 to omega-3, which include walnuts, flaxseeds, and chia seeds and their oils. However, an excessive intake of PUFAs, even healthy PUFA oils, can cause inflammation in the body, especially if they are heated. Omega-3 fats, such as DHA (docosahexaenoic acid) and EPA (eicosapentaenoic acid) found in fish and shellfish, are anti-inflammatory and quench inflammation in the body. A good ratio of omega-6 to omega-3 is 1:1 to as much as 4:1.

The main fear of patients and their physicians for decades has been saturated fats and the belief that saturated fats are the main cause of heart disease. But the truth is saturated fats only cause inflammation if they are eaten with excessive amounts of sugars or carbohydrates or if you do not consume adequate amounts of omega-3 fats, and most of us do not get adequate amounts of omega-3 fats in in our diet.

One fat that everyone should avoid is trans fat or hydrogenated fat, which promotes inflammation in the body and causes plaque to form in the arteries. I have discussed this extremely dangerous fat at length in prior books, including *The Seven Pillars of Health* and *Let Food Be Your Medicine*.

There is now a lab test that measures oxidized LDL levels. This is a much better predictor of heart disease than any other blood test. However, most physicians never order this test, maybe because there is no drug available to lower it. The Keto Zone diet will lower oxidized LDL levels as long as you lower your consumption of poly-unsaturated fats and increase your omega-3 fats.

Oxidation is technically the work of free radicals, and those free radicals are set loose to wreak havoc in our bodies by the excessive consumption of polyunsaturated fats. These free radicals cause in-flammation, and as I have told my patients for many years, inflam-mation is the root cause of most chronic diseases, including heart disease, high blood pressure, dementia, and autoimmune disease.

Jimmy Moore and Dr. Eric Westman, in *Cholesterol Clarity*, make the same call: "[Inflammation] is the real culprit in heart dis-ease, not cholesterol. Without inflammation in the body, cholester-ol would move freely through the body and never accumulate on the walls of blood vessels. Inflammation is caused when we expose our bodies to toxins or foods the human body wasn't designed to process."[31]

Eating antioxidants (such as blueberries and other berries) as well as taking antioxidant supplements such as CoQ10 and vitamin E to help combat oxidation is not a bad idea, but the way to really treat the oxidation, to wipe it out of your system, is to increase your omega-3 fats such as EPA or DHA to a healthy ratio of omega-6 to omega-3 of 4:1 or less. Choose only modest or small amounts of healthy polyunsaturated fats, such as walnuts, flaxseeds, and chia seeds, and avoid foods that contain soybean oil, corn oil, canola oil, and other inflammatory oils, especially if they are heated. Finally, by lowering your intake of sugars and starches by being in the Keto Zone, you are quenching both inflammation and oxidation.

Many foods contain soybean oil, including most margarines, shortenings, mayonnaises, salad dressings, imitation dairy, frozen foods, and commercially baked goods. Most French fries in US restaurants are cooked in corn oil, another inflammatory polyunsaturated fat that sets us up for heart disease.[32]

The Keto Zone diet plays a big role in helping treat both oxidation and inflammation.

WHAT ARE YOUR REAL CHOLESTEROL NUMBERS?

If you have taken a typical blood test, a lipid panel, you know what your LDL, HDL, and triglyceride numbers are. That is a good place to start, but there is another piece of information that may change everything for you.

On a standard lipid panel, your LDL number is technically a calculated number (the Friedewald equation). There are two types of LDL:

- Big puffy LDL pattern A (neutral)
- Small dense LDL pattern B (plaque forming)

Ratio wise, you want approximately 80 percent to be the big LDL pattern A and 20 percent or preferably less to be the small LDL pattern B. (Ideally, LDL pattern B should be less than 600 nanomoles per liter [nmol/L], but less than 200 nanomoles per liter is much better.) That is because the big pattern A LDL is not dangerous to your health. It is covered with a layer of fat, which protects it from oxidation, which in turn protects you.

It is the LDL pattern B that is dangerous. Because the small LDL pattern B is so quick to oxidize, you know that also means:

- Oxidative stress or free radicals damaging the blood vessels
- Inflammation
- Eventual plaque buildup since it can easily penetrate the wall of the artery
- Glycation or cross linking of collagen in the blood vessels, causing stiff blood vessels, more inflammation, and more plaque formation

Consider this description by Barbara V. Howard and her co-researchers: "Small LDL particles reside in the circulation longer, have greater susceptibility to oxidative damage by free radicals, and more easily penetrate the arterial wall, contributing to atherosclerosis. No matter what your total LDL-C concentration, if you have relatively more small particles (referred to as Pattern B) it puts you at a several-fold higher risk for heart disease compared to people with larger LDL particles (Pattern A)."[33]

It is sugar and carbohydrates that trigger the production of LDL pattern B cholesterol. That is because eating sugar and excessive amounts of carbohydrates (especially processed carbs) spike the blood sugar, programing the body to produce LDL pattern B cholesterol. Consider the following:

> ## IT'S A FACT
>
> High triglycerides are a sign that your LDL pattern B cholesterol is also high.

- Sugar increases free radicals in your blood.[34] And when you have free radicals, you have cell damage and organ damage, not to mention inflammation and eventually plaque accumulation in the arteries.

- "Anything that provokes an increase in blood sugar will also, in parallel, provoke small LDL particles," wrote William Davis in *Wheat Belly*. "Anything that keeps blood sugar from increasing, such as proteins, fats, and reduction in carbohydrates such as wheat, reduces small LDL particles."[35]

But when you get your cholesterol measured, most doctors will order a lipid panel test for you. This measures your combined LDL number of both pattern A and pattern B. That is like arguing that the swimming pool is completely safe for little children because it is on average only two and a half feet deep—five feet at one end and one inch at the other.

That is indeed a problem! If your LDL numbers are high, you really ought to know both of your LDL numbers, the pattern A number as well as your pattern B number. One test that gives you an accurate measurement of both your LDL numbers is the NMR (nuclear magnetic resonance) Lipoprofile. It is like an MRI profile of your cholesterol.

Most labs offer the NMR Lipoprofile test, which means it is readily available. It is helpful to have clarity on your LDL numbers. Some patients will take a lipid panel three months after starting the Keto Zone diet to see what progress they have had with their LDL. But it is a good idea, much like a second opinion, to know both LDL numbers, pattern A and pattern B. The NMR Lipoprofile, unlike a

> ### IT'S A FACT
>
> People who eat potatoes on a regular basis are at greater risk of heart disease. A study of 42 European countries found potatoes consumption to be a predictor of coronary heart disease.[36]

standard lipid panel, gives you both LDL numbers.

Your insurance may not cover the NMR Lipoprofile, but I would recommend it if you can afford it. If you cannot, have the standard lipid panel test done before you start the Keto Zone diet and then about three to six months later. Your HDL will usually go up. Your triglycerides will definitely drop, and that is good. If your overall cholesterol goes up, you really should have the NMR to see if it was the neutral LDL pattern A or the dangerous LDL pattern B that went up, then adjust the Keto Zone diet accordingly. Most commonly, the LDL pattern B goes down after three to six months on the Keto Zone diet. If your pattern B is elevated, it will usually take at least three to six months on the Keto Zone diet to lower it. (See appendix D for more information.)

STATIN DRUGS LOWER CHOLESTEROL

While many debate the side effects of statin drugs, I have seen far too many negative effects in my patients to recommend them as an effective way to lower cholesterol.

Some of the side effects of statin medication include muscle pain and damage, liver damage, increased blood sugar or type 2 diabetes, and neurological side effects including memory loss and confusion.[37]

I have personally witnessed mental deterioration in the form of memory impairment, dementia, and Alzheimer's as the direct results of cholesterol being lowered in the brain. You know how the brain needs cholesterol to function. Lowering cholesterol levels in the brain is never good, but that is one result of statin drugs.

Though the side effects are a big reason why statin drugs should rarely be used to lower cholesterol, there is also another reason.

As we have just discussed, the susceptibility of LDL pattern B to oxidize and eventually form plaque clearly puts this type at the top of the list of cholesterol you want to lower.

Everybody would agree with that, and since statin drugs lower cholesterol by as much as 40 percent, then it seems logical to get on statin drugs right away.

But based on what you now know about LDL and there being two different types, LDL pattern A and LDL pattern B, you should be asking one very important question: *Will statin drugs lower my LDL pattern B?*

Here is the problem: statin drugs do not lower LDL pattern B significantly. In fact, there is no drug to lower LDL pattern B cholesterol significantly. In one study, statin therapy did not decrease the proportion of LDL pattern B, but in fact increased it.[39]

Yes, statins lower LDL, but they are actually lowering your overall LDL number, which you know includes mainly the neutral pattern A and less of the time-bomb-ticking pattern B.

If statin drugs cannot lower your LDL pattern B significantly, why take the drug in the first place? That is a valid question, one that you will have to answer for yourself, but I do not fault the pharmaceutical companies for trying to find a medicine to reduce our

---

IT'S A FACT

Statin meds reduce levels of CoQ10 (Coenzyme Q10) in the body. CoQ10 is a powerful antioxidant that is found in almost every cell in the body and helps convert food into energy. Studies have shown that CoQ10 may decrease the muscle pain from statin meds.[38] Patients on statin meds should take 100 milligrams of CoQ10 once or twice a day.

cholesterol problems. What they did not know when they started, as we have only discovered in the past twenty years or so, is that LDL is composed of two very different numbers and that it is the LDL pattern B that causes us untold troubles. Statin drugs do decrease inflammation, which is one of the root causes of heart disease.

The low-fat, high-carb mind-set from the 1950s was also based on insufficient evidence. Saturated fats, almost a swear word in some circles, do indeed raise cholesterol—LDL pattern A, the neutral kind. But it is the excessive sugars and carbs that mainly raise the dangerous LDL pattern B cholesterol.

All the fear about fats clogging arteries and causing heart attacks turns out to be unfounded. That revelation is a game changer for many.

The fact that statin drugs cannot lower LDL pattern B significantly explains a few things, such as: why heart disease has only continued to climb despite the high number of prescriptions for statins, why many heart attack victims had healthy levels of LDL, and why lower LDL numbers do not equal a lower risk for heart attacks.

That also explains why countries like France, which consumes far more fat (especially olive oil) than the United States, and Switzerland, which has significantly higher cholesterol rates than the United States, both have much lower rates of heart disease and heart attacks than the United States.[40]

With all that said, it is clearly no longer a question about lowering cholesterol in general. Instead, there is only one question that we all (doctors included) should be concerned with: *How can I lower my LDL pattern B?*

The good news is that your LDL pattern B can be lowered by reducing your intake of carbs and sugars. And that reality brings us right back to the Keto Zone diet.

THE KETO ZONE DIET AT WORK

The Keto Zone diet effectively lowers your triglycerides, raises your HDL, lowers your LDL pattern B, and usually either lowers, maintains, or raises the neutral LDL pattern A. More specifically, it helps convert your LDL pattern B into pattern A. (See appendix D for more information.)

It is pretty amazing that it is possible to change the dangerous small LDL pattern B into neutral large LDL pattern A, but that is exactly what happens on a low-carb diet.[41]

As for lowering the triglyceride levels, those are specifically impacted by the low-carb diet. As Jeff Volek and Stephen Phinney explain, "When our metabolism adapts to a low carbohydrate diet, saturated fats become a preferred fuel for the body, and their levels in blood and tissue triglyceride pools actually drop."[42]

IT'S A FACT

It's not dietary fat that causes high triglycerides— it's carbs and sugars.

Clearly, a low-carb diet is the best plan of attack for better heart health. The healthy high-fat and moderate-protein elements of the Keto Zone diet also help significantly, specifically with fish oil (omega-3), olive oil, almonds, pecans, macadamia nuts, avocados, grass-fed butter, and grass-fed meats, but we will talk more about those specific foods soon.

Many people have high triglycerides, low HDL, and high LDL. It is extremely common. That is also a sign they have elevated amounts of LDL pattern B hard at work forming plaque. They need to take action, and the Keto Zone diet is the answer.

The Keto Zone diet will help your body convert the small LDL pattern B particles into the big neutral LDL pattern A. At the same time, your HDL numbers usually go up, and your triglyceride levels almost always go down (as does your blood pressure).

And you will lose unwanted weight along the way—all the better!

"When I fully understood
what the Keto Zone diet
does for my body,
I was sold."
—*Dean*

CHAPTER SEVEN

THE KETO ZONE AND YOUR CARBOHYDRATES

The Keto Zone Diet: **LOW-CARB**, High-Fat, Moderate-Protein

SUSAN WAS ONLY THIRTY-ONE YEARS OLD, but she was tired all the time. Whether she was at work or at home, she felt exhausted and always in need of a nap despite getting eight hours of sleep a night. Sure, she had two young children, but her fatigue was more than that.

When she visited my office, she was a little obese (she said she wanted to lose thirty pounds), but her chief concern was the ever-increasing feelings of tiredness. She had interests and hobbies she wanted to pursue, but after work and tucking her two girls into bed, she was ready for bed herself. She wondered if her thyroid might be acting up or if she was deficient in a specific mineral or vitamin. We talked about her eating habits and other patterns that might play a part.

"There is no pill or supplement that will fix this," I explained. "What you are experiencing is your body being exhausted from adrenal fatigue."

Like so many mothers with young children, she was on the sugar-carb roller coaster. When her energy was low, she would reach for a soda, candy bar, donut, or expensive mocha coffee and get a brief burst of energy from her sugar high. Then after a couple of hours her blood sugar would crash again, leaving her irritable, tired, hungry, and looking for her next sugar or carb fix.

After spending months on this sugar roller coaster, she eventually became chronically fatigued and no longer experienced the sugar high. Susan had developed adrenal fatigue, and every time she experienced low blood sugar, figuratively speaking, more energy was sapped from her adrenal bank account until she was overdrawn and always exhausted.

> **IT'S A FACT**
>
> Eating carbs and sugars only makes you hungrier.

She looked at me like I was the one confused, so I continued: "Your body is producing large amounts of adrenaline to try to raise your blood sugar when you are tired, hungry, and irritable. This is like a metabolic marathon for your body, followed by a short break, then another marathon, off and on all day long. With meals and snacks, this happens five or six times a day at least. Your body is tired, probably running at less than 50 percent of its potential."

She nodded in agreement and added, "I do feel like I'm running on empty."

After I explained the value and power of the Keto Zone diet, she was especially interested in the increased energy side of things. Six weeks later, I was not surprised at all to hear she was a bustling ball of momentum.

"I don't know what happened to me!" she exclaimed. "I not only have energy, I feel good. I feel like my brain and my body are both engaged for the first time in a long time. I'm exercising again, doing things I want to do, because I don't know what to do with all my energy!"

I have had a lot of patients like Susan over the years. They are not all that interested in facts and details about the body having limitless fuel to burn in the Keto Zone diet as compared to the usual high-carb diet that burns sugars as fuel. They are, however, extremely interested in getting their lives back. Details aside, they simply want the energy.

No, they may not suffer from a disease, but their lives are not what they could be. It is incredibly gratifying to see them get back in their own groove of living life as they want.

CARBS, STARCHES, AND SUGARS

Everything you just learned in the last chapter about cholesterol and oxidation, inflammation, and all those chronic diseases is also relevant here. That is because the real culprit behind heart disease is excessive intake of polyunsaturated fats and sugar, and excessive carbohydrates and starches that become sugar in your body.

You may have heard sugars described as monosaccharides ("simple sugars") and disaccharides. Monosaccharides contain one sugar such as glucose, fructose, or galactose, and disaccharides contain two sugars such as lactose (milk sugar) and sucrose (the normal sugar we use).

Starches are considered to be "complex" because they are made of long glucose chains (polysaccharides), but after digestion they are eventually broken down to glucose. Common starches include cereals, breads, rice, pasta, corn, wheat, and potatoes.

That is for many the most catastrophic news ever. Look at it this way:

- Sugar is sugar.
- Carbohydrates are eventually converted to sugar.
- Starches are eventually converted to sugar.

In your body, whether it is a sugar, carb, or starch, it all registers as a sugar in the end.

Of course, not every carb, starch, or sugar is created equal. By its nature, everything you eat has a value or number associated with it. For example, 12 ounces of green leafy vegetables have a lower carb value (glycemic index) than 12 ounces of potatoes, and 12 ounces of bread have a different carb value than 12 ounces of cheese.

> **IT'S A FACT**
>
> "Wheat and related grains are potent appetite stimulants."[43]
> —William Davis, author of *Wheat Belly*

Maybe you have heard of "net carbs." That number is achieved by subtracting fiber carbs from total carbs. A few nuts, for example, may have a total of 10 carbs, but with 5 fiber carbs, the net carb value is going to be 5. Knowing the net carbs of food can help you choose the best carbs for losing weight.

The point is, if you are eating a lot of carbs and starches, your body is getting a lot more sugar than you might think. I have patients describe what they usually eat, and sometimes 90 percent of what they eat falls into the sugar-carb-starch category.

Take a moment and consider these healthy foods that get many of us up and out the door every morning:

- Freshly squeezed orange juice
- Oatmeal with raisins
- Whole-wheat French toast

- Banana nut muffins
- Bagels with cream cheese
- Fresh fruit
- Juiced carrots
- Cereal

Sadly, everything here falls into the sugar-carb-starch category. Not because it is unhealthy, bad, or dripping with sugars like icing, frosting, donuts, syrup, or jam, but because your body eventually converts it all to sugar. The 8 ounces of 100 percent natural orange juice, which I used to drink every single morning, is still mainly sugar.

When I explain this to my patients, some of them, with a look of dismay on their faces, explain, "But I'm not eating donuts every day for breakfast!" Though that is true, our bodies convert donuts or bread or oatmeal or fresh fruit into sugar.

> ### IT'S A FACT
> Most agave syrup has a higher fructose content than even high fructose corn syrup (HFCS). HFCS has about 55 percent fructose content, whereas agave has 55 to 97 percent.

For processed foods, the combined sugar content is even worse. Back in the 1980s and 1990s when food manufacturers reformulated their products to remove much of the fat, sugar was one of the key replacement ingredients. Processed sugars, such as high fructose corn syrup, are far worse on your body than natural sugar is.

As for sodas, ice cream, candy, and cakes, you would expect them to contain a lot of sugar. That is not surprising. It is the healthy and natural foods that often trip us up. When we become aware of what we are eating, even if it is healthy sugars, we start to see just how much sugar is included.

Whether it is a sugar, carbs, or starches, your body converts it all to glucose to burn as fuel. Any and all excess glucose is stored as glycogen (in the liver and muscles) or fat. Odds are, especially if we are anywhere close to the USDA diet recommendations, we are getting much more sugar than we need.

If you are trying to lose weight, all of this comes into play. That is because your body can burn off excess fat when you lower your carb intake enough.

LOW-CARB FOR WEIGHT LOSS

We have all heard about essential vitamins and minerals that our bodies need every day for good health and peak performance. All advertising aside, here are the essentials for fats and proteins:

- *Fats:* Your body only needs two specific fatty acids. These cannot be made by your body, so you must get them from the foods you eat. These two essential fatty acids are linoleic acid (omega-6) and alpha-linolenic acid (omega-3).
- *Protein:* Your body needs nine specific amino acids. These also cannot be made by your body, so you must obtain them from the foods you eat. These nine essential amino acids are histidine, isoleucine, leucine, lysine, methionine, phenylalanine, threonine, tryptophan, and valine.

Did you notice something? *There are no essential carbohydrates.* For health and life, you need certain proteins and fats, but your body does not technically need any carbohydrates (or sugars or carbs or starches). For enjoyment, yes, we want our sweets and breads and such, but it is not necessary for living. That is something to think about.

Our normal low-fat, high-carb diet provides us with too much of what we do not actually need. With starches and carbs as the base of the food pyramid, what do you expect, right? The average person clocks in around 200 to 300 grams of carbs a day.

As we have already mentioned, everyone has a specific ideal carb management number. Quite simply, eating more carbohydrates than that number equals weight gain; eating less equals weight loss.

I call this ideal carb management number your KCL, or Keto Carb Limit. Your KCL may be 20 grams or 50 grams or 75 grams or 100 grams per day. Nobody knows, but you will find your KCL as you put the Keto Zone diet to work in your life.

Finding your KCL is vitally important to your long-term weight loss and long-term health. For now, though, it is pretty safe to assume your KCL is usually somewhere between 20 and 100 grams per day.

> **IT'S A FACT**
>
> A carb that is void of nutritional value is "carbage."
>
> —term coined by Jimmy Moore, author of *Cholesterol Clarity* and *Keto Clarity*

Some people, for one reason or another, have a much lower KCL than the rest of us. I know one individual whose KCL is a mere 10 grams per day. That is extremely low, but if he exceeds it, he gains weight. He also used to suffer from a lot of allergic reactions and inflammation, which is part of the reason why 10 grams per day of carbs is his KCL.

If you are carbohydrate sensitive and insulin resistant, your KCL might temporarily be lower than what it will be for the long term.

Usually, by lowering your insulin levels, which happens on the

Keto Zone diet, your body will eventually resensitize to insulin. Call it a reboot if you will, likely enabling your body to get back to its ideal KCL number.

For example, if your body can handle 50 grams of carbs per day without gaining weight, that is your KCL and that will be where you end up. If your body can only handle 20 grams per day, perhaps due to carb sensitivity, insulin resistance, pre-diabetes, or type 2 diabetes, then to lose weight you simply need to lower your carb count below 20 grams.

Once you have burned off the fat and reached your desired weight, you will usually have a new KCL number. Maybe it will be 50 grams or 75 grams or 100 grams or some other number. It will usually be higher than the fat-burning 20 grams.

IT'S A FACT

Carbohydrate Sensitivity and Insulin Resistance

- Most people build up a sensitivity to carbs as they age.
- Carb sensitivity brings on insulin resistance, which means more insulin is needed to counterbalance carb intake.
- Insulin resistance leads to weight gain, especially belly fat.
- Appetite hormones are eventually scrambled.
- Constant hunger usually occurs.
- Metabolism slows down. Fat burning is almost impossible.
- Obesity, metabolic syndrome, pre-diabetes, type 2 diabetes, heart disease, and other diseases begin to develop.
- Men with a 40-inch waist and women with a 35-inch waist are usually carb sensitive and insulin resistant.

(See chapter 3 for more details.)

The Keto Zone diet, to kick things into high gear, drops the KCL down to a mere 20 grams per day. Why? Simply because that number should be sufficiently lower than almost everyone's ideal long-term KCL number, and that means immediate weight loss.

THE BUMPY ROAD OF CARBS

Our bodies store only a small amount of carbs as glycogen (on average, 1,500 to 2,000 calories) in the liver and muscles. However, our bodies store a lot more fat. Extra carbs are usually converted to fat, but since our usual diet is not low enough in carbs to burn off the fat, the fat likely never goes away. It steadily increases.

The cycle of carbs, and sugars and starches for that matter, is simple. It goes like this:

1. You eat carbs and your blood glucose levels rise.
2. Your pancreas pumps out more insulin to lower your blood sugar levels.
3. Over time, the increased insulin pumped out, repeatedly throughout the day to handle the spikes in sugar, eventually causes insulin resistance, and both insulin and sugar levels rise in the blood, triggering even more weight gain.
4. Meanwhile, the carbs are burned for fuel or stored as fat, and with excess consumption of carbs and increased insulin resistance, the fat-storage process speeds up as we age.

The inevitable path of a high-carb diet is one that leads directly to all the chronic diseases, including obesity, heart disease, type 2 diabetes, dementia, autoimmune disorders, hypertension, and more. Thankfully, that is not the path you have to take!

Carbohydrates also have the distinction of doing things to your body that you do not want, such as:

- Slowing your metabolism
- Causing high insulin levels, programming you for fat storage and stopping or slowing down most fat burning
- Flooding your bloodstream with triglycerides[44]
- Greasing the slope to eventually developing thirty-five epidemic yet preventable diseases
- Increasing appetite and food cravings
- Causing a fatty liver, which affects your liver's ability to detoxify, leading to a buildup of toxins and increasing fatigue

IT'S A FACT

Finding your KCL (Keto Carb Limit) draws the line in the sand for weight loss and ideal health. If you reduce your carb intake below your ideal KCL, you will lose weight. It is inevitable.

The famous political thinker Edmund Burke (1729–97) once said, "Those who don't know history are destined to repeat it." I would change this a bit to: *Those who don't lower their carb intake are destined to never lose weight.*

Sugars, carbs, and starches are literally the only real obstacle between you and your desired weight. Get rid of sugars, starches, and excessive carbs and all this is a nonissue.

Reality, however, is another matter. Carbs are an integral part of our world.

Yes, lowering carb intake below your KCL is the secret to your weight loss, accomplished through the Keto Zone diet, but it is going to take some work on your part.

Yes, lowering insulin (the hormone that programs your body to store fat) levels by lowering carb intake is the only way to burn excess fat over the long term, and that is the goal here. It is still going to take effort.

You can do it. All of it is possible.

The answer is taking action in a way that accomplishes your goals, such as weight loss, increased energy, mental clarity, health, or disease prevention, while at the same time following a plan that you can live with and do on a daily basis.

It must be doable, manageable, and effective.

The Keto Zone diet is just that.

"The Keto Zone diet
is a shockingly easy way to burn fat.
I was losing fat so fast
I could not believe it was happening."
—*Kyle*

CHAPTER EIGHT

THE KETO ZONE AND YOUR FAT

The Keto Zone Diet: Low-Carb, **HIGH-FAT**, Moderate-Protein

I HELPED JEFFREY LOSE THIRTY POUNDS with an anti-inflammatory diet, but he wanted to turn things up a notch. He needed to lose more weight, and he had a few health issues, all of which would be addressed by the Keto Zone diet.

Together, we went to a nearby grocery store. I showed him what to buy: grass-fed butter, olive oil, grass-fed beef, avocados, different nuts and nut butters, powdered MCT oil (a special oil, medium-chain triglyceride, that helps you break into the Keto Zone quickly), coconut oil, a bunch of green veggies, pastured eggs (from free-range chickens), and several other items, including a few spices. When we were done, I went over the diet with him and then headed to my car.

On my drive home, I suddenly realized I had failed to read his body language. I thought he was rushing through the store because he had other things to do, but in fact he was objecting to what I was telling him to buy.

I had scared him to death!

Jeffrey was sixty years old and had heard probably a thousand times, "If you eat fats, you'll eventually drop dead from a heart attack." Putting the grass-fed butter in his shopping cart, his hands seemed to be trembling. The cartons of pastured eggs were just too much. He was afraid I was trying to kill him!

The next day I called and gave him additional research to show that some fats are friends and some are enemies. He had a hard time believing me, and I knew why. He suffered from fat phobia, as do 90 percent or more of my patients. The remaining 10 percent are usually too sick and have a greater fear of death than they do of fat.

For Jeffrey, I knew that until he got past the fear of fat, the Keto Zone diet would do him no good because he would not even be willing to start it.

> ### IT'S A FACT
> Saturated fats do not cause plaque in arteries. It is oxidization of LDL cholesterol and excessive consumption of sugars and carbs that mainly cause plaque.

FAT . . . FRIEND OR FOE?

Basically, everything we are told about fat boils down to this: it's bad for us. Medical doctors often recommend a low-fat diet. Almost every health industry, regulation, and review board warns about the dangers of fat. Even young children somehow believe this to be true.

But you know better. Based on everything you have learned so far, look again at these valid concerns:

Fear: Fat causes cancer.
Fact: Sugar feeds cancer cells and causes inflammation, which is behind almost every chronic disease.

Fear: Fat causes obesity.

Fact: Excessive sugar and carb consumption cause obesity.

Fear: Fat clogs your arteries.

Fact: Plaque buildup is mainly from increased LDL pattern B cholesterol caused by too much sugar and carbs, and from oxidized cholesterol caused by consuming too many polyunsaturated fats.

Fear: Fat causes heart disease.

Fact: Most cardiovascular disease is due to inflammation and elevated LDL pattern B, which is triggered by excessive sugar and carb intake.

Fear: Saturated fat raises cholesterol levels.

Fact: Saturated fats raise the neutral LDL pattern A cholesterol and the healthy HDL cholesterol, but sugar and carbs raise the unhealthy LDL pattern B cholesterol.

Fear: Fat makes you fat.

Fact: Fat is formed from extra carbs and sugars not used for fuel. These are converted to fat in the liver and stored in the body. Excessive insulin production from eating sugars and carbs promotes fat storage, especially belly fat. So eating too many carbs, starches, and sugars is what causes most body fat.

Over time, misleading information from countless sources has caused us to believe that fat, especially saturated fat, is bad. Fears have become facts. Once that happens, there is very little you can say or do to refute it. "You can't argue with the facts," people say. The problem is that their facts are not true.

Here are a few more facts to consider:

- "Cutting fat does not reduce the risk of heart disease. In fact, eating a low-fat diet causes incredible metabolic distortions, like high blood sugar, hyperglycemia, rising fasting glucose, insulin resistance, growth of belly fat, hypertension, metabolic syndrome, and diabetes in the genetically susceptible," wrote William Davis, author of *Wheat Belly*.

- A massive study, The Women's Health Initiative, lasting eight years, costing more than four hundred million dollars, and measuring almost fifty thousand women, published its findings in the February 7, 2006, *Journal of the American Medical Association*. The conclusion: a low-fat diet does not prevent heart disease.

- "The current scientific consensus is that total fat in your diet does not affect your risk of heart disease or being overweight," wrote Mark Hyman, author of *Eat Fat, Get Thin*, "and yet many doctors and dieticians still hold on to this outdated idea."

- One twenty-year study of eighty thousand women found no connection between fat intake and weight gain.[45]

- Another study of forty-three thousand men found no connection between dietary fat or saturated fat and heart disease.[46]

This fear of fat is indeed an obstacle for almost all of us. Honestly, I used to suffer from fat phobia myself. I think everyone does to some degree, unless we grew up in parts of the world where people, like the Inuit in northern Canada, understood fat to be a necessary and healthy part of life.

But rest assured, though the Keto Zone diet is low-carb, high-

> ### IT'S A FACT
> Saturated fats burn quickly in a low-carb body.

fat, and moderate-protein, it is also healthy and the best weight-loss method in the world.

So, what is your answer? Is fat a friend or foe?

Without question, it is your friend!

WHAT IS FAT FOR?

The fact that the Keto Zone diet is "high-fat" does not mean you eat butter by the stick or that you drink bottles of oil. Nor does it require you to eat pounds of fried greasy foods or cook everything in lard.

To begin with, and perhaps to calm some persistent fat-phobia alarms that may be ringing in the back of your head, it is important to recognize the primary value of fat.

In the form of oils, butters, meats, nuts, and fish, the high-fat part of the Keto Zone diet accomplishes two main goals:

1. *To satisfy you:* These foods make you feel full, satisfied, without cravings or hunger, and happy for many hours.
2. *To nourish you:* These foods provide your body with the essential fatty acids, fat-soluble vitamins, and healthy fats in the correct ratios that will decrease inflammation

in the body. (According to the 2005 Dietary Guidelines of America, a low intake of fats, less than 20 percent of calories, increases the risk of not getting enough vitamin E and the two essential fats.)

That is what fat is for, in a nutshell. Of course there are more details to learn and apply, but that is the reasoning behind the high-fat part of the Keto Zone diet.

Nobody I know objects to feeling satisfied and being nourished, especially while on a fat-burning diet.

FATS ARE CONFUSING

Part of the phobia around fats is no doubt connected to the overall confusion about fats: the names, what is natural, what is manmade, where it comes from, and whether it is inflammatory or anti-inflammatory.

For example, fish oil (which is good for you) and corn oil (which is not good for you) are both polyunsaturated fats. How is anyone supposed to know which fats are healthy and which are not?

In the world of fats, you have these four main groupings:

1. Saturated fats
2. Monounsaturated fats
3. Polyunsaturated fats
4. Trans fats

Each fat has specific fats within each group, some with their own unique name. Palm oil, for example, is a saturated fat called palmitate, while cocoa butter, also a saturated fat, is composed primarily of stearate. Also, at the cellular level, each fat affects the body in a different way. For the sake of clarity, the Keto Zone diet uses the general name, such as coconut oil, rather than mentioning the fact that coconut oil is a combination of mainly two fats, laurate and myristate.

Then, to add another layer of confusion to the mix, is all the marketing that tries to convince us that this oil is better, this spread is best, this spritzer is optimum, this butter beats them all, and so on. Whom do you believe?

One way to make sense of it all is to look at your own body. At the cellular level, your cells are made up of fats. These fatty acids that make up your cells consist of saturated fats, monounsaturated fats, and a small amount of polyunsaturated fats. It looks like this:

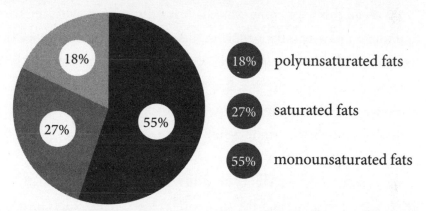

Because our cells are made up of fats, the health of those fats directly affects our own health. Remember that oxidation, like rusting, of the dangerous LDL pattern B cholesterol occurs much more quickly and easily than it does with the neutral LDL pattern A. What provides a protective layer around the LDL pattern A is a thin layer of fat.

We need a balance of fats in our body. That is partly why a low-fat diet is inherently unhealthy. Deprive your body and brain of fats, especially in your brain, and you will eventually have a host of problems. After all, your brain is about 60 percent fat, and a significant amount of the brain is composed of cholesterol, omega-3 fats, and phospholipids.

Back in your cells, the healthy foods and fats you eat help provide the cell membranes with stiffness and structure (from saturated fats) and flexibility (from the polyunsaturated fats in fish oil). Dietary fats help regulate inflammation and improve brain function and mood.

Unhealthy foods and fats cause the cell membrane to become more porous, unstable, and floppy. The cells do not function well, and conditions are ideal for free radical damage, inflammation, and oxidation. This eventually leads directly to sickness and disease.

With all this happening behind closed doors, as it were, it is easy to understand why most people in the grocery aisle do not have the time or the interest to mess with conflicting facts about oils, fats, butters, spreads, and the like. It is far easier to take the low-fat route and try to avoid everything fatty.

As you know, that route is not really an option.

FATS YOUR BODY NEEDS

There are two yogurts on the shelf: one is low-fat and high in sugar while the other is low in sugar yet high-fat. Most people would automatically choose the low-fat option without blinking, but when you consider insulin spikes, fat storage, and the body's need for healthy fats, which would you choose?

For most of my patients, knowing the reason why certain fats are recommended, healthy, and necessary helps them shift out of their fat-phobia thinking. It helped me.

When it comes to the Keto Zone diet, it also helps to know in advance that the fats (in oils, butters, and meats) in the diet are there to provide you, all the way down to your cells, with the fuel your body needs to function at its peak performance. Your dietary fat becomes your fuel. You are no longer burning sugar as your fuel.

For example, you could honestly call this a brain-food diet because the fats you eat usually bring such clear thinking and focus that you will be amazed. The mental fog that may plague you, as it does millions of people every day, usually burns away so you can be bright-eyed and alert.

> **IT'S A FACT**
>
> Saturated fats from grass-fed animals raise HDL, which helps remove the plaque from the arteries.

The truth remains that your body needs certain fats—not every fat, nor in large quantities, but the right fats (that are healthy) and in the right amount. That is partly what makes the Keto Zone diet so unique and powerful.

Here is a more careful look at the four fats and how they affect you:

SATURATED FATS

Saturated fats, often maligned and mislabeled as the "killer" fat, are still only marginally accepted. The 2015–2020 Dietary Guidelines for Americans says that saturated fats should be less than 10 percent of total daily caloric intake. I disagree, but I do recommend that saturated fats be balanced with monounsaturated fats or that your diet have slightly more monounsaturated fats.[47] Remember the fatty acid composition of our cell is 55 percent monounsaturated fats and only 27 percent saturated fats.

Saturated fats include coconut oil, palm oil, grass-fed butter, and cocoa butter. Eating more of these will help you:

- Decrease inflammation[48]
- Boost brain function and decrease dementia risk[49]

On the Keto Zone diet, I recommend using coconut oil for cooking, such as when frying an egg or sautéing vegetables. Grass-fed butter or ghee (clarified butter) also works for frying as well as a host of other uses. Do not fry with olive oil, avocado oil, or other monounsaturated fats. Never fry with polyunsaturated fats such as corn oil, soybean oil, grapeseed oil, safflower oil, sunflower oil, etc., since those fats produce excessive inflammatory lipid peroxides.

Do you remember how insulin spikes when we eat carbs, sugars, and starches and how the insulin shuts down the fat-burning process? Well, interestingly, when you are in the Keto Zone, fats have no effect on your blood glucose levels or your insulin levels. There are no insulin spikes and none of the negatives that come with it. Instead, you have a steady, satisfied, full feeling.

MONOUNSATURATED FATS

Most monounsaturated fats are healthy, with the primary one being olive oil. Others include avocado oil, almond oil, quite a few nuts—including almonds, pecans, and macadamia nuts. (Eating the whole olive, avocado, and nuts is fine as well.) Some monounsaturated fats are also found in lard, tallow (sheep and beef fat), many dairy products, and grass-fed beef, goat, and sheep.

Technically, olive oil is a mixture of oils (75 percent monounsaturated, 13 percent saturated, and 12 percent polyunsaturated), but to keep it simple, it is called a monounsaturated fat (further proof that fats can be confusing). I prefer organic extra-virgin olive oil and unrefined, cold-pressed organic extra-virgin avocado oil.

You will notice on the Keto Zone diet that some monounsaturated fats are not included or are discouraged. That is for two reasons. First, the goal is to stay in the Keto Zone so that ketone production is going full force and you are burning fat, and some sources of monounsaturated fats (e.g., cashews), though healthy, have enough carbs to bump you out of the Keto Zone. Second, some monounsaturated fats, such as grass-fed butter, are better for long-term health than others, such as lard. The monounsaturated fat that I warn patients to avoid is canola oil, because approximately 90 percent of it is genetically modified and because it is usually partially hydrogenated.

> ### IT'S A FACT
> Monounsaturated help fight arthritis, lower risk of strokes, and reduce breast cancer risks.

Overall, monounsaturated fats are very good for you because they help:

- Lower inflammation to help with arthritis[50]
- Lessen your chances for strokes[51]
- Reduce breast cancer risk[52]
- Raise the protective HDL cholesterol

Grass-fed meats (beef, lamb, goat, and wild game like deer, elk, moose, and antelope) have more monounsaturated fats, nutrients, and vitamins than grain-fed meats, as do their grass-fed animal products like butter, cheese, milk, and yogurt.

When it comes to grass-fed versus grain-fed animals, the fat composition is markedly different. The grass-fed contains more nutrients and vitamins. Remember the "peculiar" anthropologist Stefansson who checked himself into a NYC hospital and ate only meat and drank only water for a year was declared perfectly healthy with no deficiencies, high blood pressure, scurvy, hair loss, or negative side effects at all.

What is more, farm-raised animals get their fair share of antibiotics, pesticides, estrogen and other hormones, and "other" ingredients (including sawdust, candy, candy wrappers, chicken poop, and fish guts).[53]

Whether the animal fattens up for market or produces more milk, any toxins from mold, GMO feed, bovine growth hormones,[54] bovine estrogen, pesticides, and the like end up generally being stored in the animal's fatty tissue, which then passes to us through the meats and dairy products we eat.

With cancer patients, I found those who ate grain-fed meat as part of their diet actually got sicker. The meats had toxins, so I reduced their intake and increased grass-fed butters and small amounts of grass-fed meats, and we had much better results.

POLYUNSATURATED FATS

Polyunsaturated fats are found in corn oil, sunflower oil, cottonseed oil, sesame oil, safflower oil, soybean oil, grape-seed oil, and flaxseed oil. Certain seeds (pumpkin, sesame, chia, sunflower), fish (wild salmon, herring, sardines, mackerel, trout, anchovies, tuna), and walnuts also have polyunsaturated fats.

This is where things get interesting. As you know, there are only two essential fatty acids our bodies need: linoleic acid (omega-6) and alpha-linolenic acid (omega-3). Both happen to be in the polyunsaturated fat group.

There are literally hundreds of primary and secondary benefits from these essential fatty acids. A few include:

- Healthy cell membranes
- Healthy blood clotting
- Hormone production
- Healthy brain function
- Skin and hair health
- Reproductive system health
- Healthy metabolism
- Healthy thyroid
- Breakdown and transport of cholesterol
- Healthy immune system

No doubt you want those! However, most of us typically get way too much omega-6 in our diets, and conversely, few of us get enough omega-3. The ideal ratio would be 1:1 to 4:1 (omega-6 to omega-3), but some people are reportedly so out of balance that their ratio climbs as high as 25:1 or even 50:1.

This imbalance causes, among other things, heart disease, cancer, autoimmune disease, and inflammation.[55] It also creates blood clots, blocks the uptake of good omega-3, causes the blood to get sticky, and causes LDL cholesterol to oxidize, setting the stage for plaque forming in the arteries.

When you realize how good omega-3 is for your body, the fact

> **IT'S A FACT**
>
> Beware: soybean oil is the most common type of oil used in the production of salad dressings.

that it is blocked by too much omega-6 is by itself sufficient reason to work to adjust the imbalanced ratio. Omega-3 fat helps fight cancer (breast, colon, and prostate), asthma, IBS, ADHD, depression, memory loss, loss of eyesight, arthritis, diabetes, heart disease, high blood pressure, high cholesterol, and more.[56]

The problem is that omega-6 is almost everywhere. Most snack foods and fast foods contain omega-6. In fact, according to Dr. Andrew Weil, "Soybean oil alone is now so ubiquitous in fast foods and processed foods that an astounding 20 percent of the calories in the American diet are estimated to come from this single source."[57]

The fact that the 2015 Dietary Guidelines Advisory Committee recommends using soybean, corn, and canola oils rather than butter, cream, or coconut oils does not help either. Too much polyunsaturated fat intake only feeds the imbalance, fueling inflammation and the resulting diseases all the more.

There is no recommended standard dose of omega-3 fats a day, but I usually recommend for my patients to take 1 to 2 grams total a day of DHA and EPA in the form of krill oil or fish oil or a combination of both. (Krill oil may be better absorbed than fish oil.) As a supplement, this is very easy to do. Eating wild salmon is another great way to get your omega-3. (See appendix A for more information.)

Clearly, eating a 1:1 to 4:1 ratio of omega-6 to omega-3 is a challenge. When you get on the Keto Zone diet, you need to clear out and restock your cupboards and pantry with foods that are healthy and keep you in the Keto Zone.

TRANS FATS

Grass-fed butter is actually good for you. A single tablespoon of grass-fed butter contains high amounts of vitamin A, carotenes, vitamin D, vitamin E, and vitamin K_2. And yet people often choose margarine, which has been shown to cause heart attacks, increase blood insulin levels, decrease HDL, and much more.[58]

Margarines, donuts, French fries, and host of other foods, especially processed foods, contain trans fats that have been repeatedly shown to increase the dangerous LDL pattern B and lower HDL (the good cholesterol); to cause heart disease, dementia, weight gain, belly fat, obesity, insulin resistance, and type 2 diabetes; and to possibly increase the risk of cancer.

The FDA banned trans fats in 2015, yet processed food companies can have up to 0.5 grams of trans fat per serving and still have "0 grams trans fat" on the label.[59]

Simply put, trans fats offer you nothing of value and cause tremendous harm. Sadly, a new fat is being used as trans fats are fading out. These new fats are IE (interesterified fats) and were developed to take the place of trans fats in snack foods and baked goods. Now food labels can tout "zero trans fats" but have IE fats, which are just as dangerous.

Research published in *Nutrition and Metabolism* found that IE fats raise the LDL cholesterol, lower the good HDL cholesterol, and raise after-meal glucose (blood sugar) by a whopping 40 percent, but there is no labeling available to warn consumers about a product containing IE fats. These IE fats are found in many prepackaged foods, baked goods, restaurant foods, and snack foods, but can be avoided by consuming natural foods.[60]

As a result of the IE-fat manufacturing process, the oil goes

> **IT'S A FACT**
>
> When you burn fat for fuel, you lose weight. If you burn sugars for fuel, you usually gain weight.

rancid more slowly, which makes it well suited for deep frying and making margarine. It tastes good and has a low saturated fat content. However, many physicians are warning that IE fats are worse than trans fats since they increase the risk of heart disease, stroke, and diabetes, whereas trans fats increase the risk of mainly cardio-vascular disease and stroke.

Since the FDA ordered food companies to eliminate trans fats entirely by June 2018, processed-food companies have been scrambling for a replacement. IE fats are one replacement, but they will not appear on the label. Instead, manufacturers may use terms such as "high stearate" or "stearic rich." If the label of a processed food has "vegetable oil" on its label of ingredients, then you most likely are consuming either IE fats or trans fats.[61]

WHAT TO EXPECT ON THE KETO ZONE DIET

When women lose weight, they sometimes lose weight in the face and look gaunt. I have seen that many times with extreme low-fat diets. The Keto Zone diet, however, targets belly fat. Your face may lose a little weight as you lose belly fat and body fat, but looking gaunt will not be a concern.

In a slightly ironic way, the fats we consume on the Keto Zone diet have everything to do with the following:

- Fitting in those jeans again
- Losing weight
- Wearing that dress
- Feeling good
- Being healthy
- Living longer
- Suffering fewer illnesses

- Looking good
- Staying active
- Lowering cholesterol
- Avoiding disease

As for how much oil, butter, fish, nuts, and meat are ideal to get you into the Keto Zone and burn off excess fat, the answer is balanced and healthy amount.

The ratio of saturated to monounsaturated fats is close to 1:1, so if you eat a tablespoon of grass-fed butter, offset it with a tablespoon of olive oil, avocado oil, or a handful of almonds, pecans, or macadamia nuts (raw nuts are best, but roasted are fine). This 50/50 approach also offers you more food options. (For people with high cholesterol or those who are working to lower their cholesterol, a 20/80 ratio may be necessary. Appendix D outlines this in greater detail.)

The diet is also flexible in that if you find yourself still hungry, you can increase your fat intake a bit. This is vital for the Keto Zone diet because:

The only reason people fall out of the Keto Zone is because they're not eating enough fats and are eating too much protein or too many carbs.

If you need to increase your fats (saturated or monounsaturated), that is fine. It is not going to hurt you because you have decreased your sugar and carb intake so much that excessive oxidation, inflammation, or insulin spikes will not occur.

The caloric intake of the Keto Zone diet consists of:

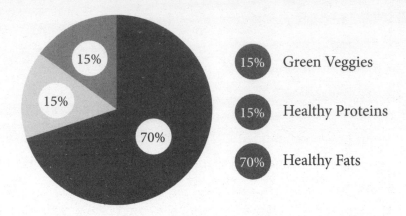

15%   Green Veggies

15%   Healthy Proteins

70%   Healthy Fats

This is flexible in that if you need to increase fats a bit more or decrease proteins, or even eat more green veggies, you will usually remain in the Keto Zone. The 20 grams of carbs usually should not be increased until your desired weight is achieved.

How much fat is 70 percent of your diet? We are only talking about approximately 8 to 10 tablespoons of fat per day for men, 6 to 8 tablespoons a day for women, and sometimes more. With the menus and recipes in the following chapters, this will be incredibly easy to accomplish. And you will usually feel full all day and all night as a result, while losing weight.

Breaking it down, if 2,000 calories per day is average for men, then that is about 140 grams of fat (.07 x 2,000). Each tablespoon of oil is about 14 grams of fat, so that is approximately 10 tablespoons a day. (A gram of fat is technically 9 calories, but rounding it up to 10 calories per gram makes for easier math.) An approximate 1,500 calorie intake for women results in 6 to 8 tablespoons of fat a day.

If you really want to lower the dangerous LDL pattern B, or had an NMR Lipoprofile that showed more LDL pattern B than you would like, you can adjust the fat ratio to 25 to 50 percent saturated fats and 50 to 75 percent monounsaturated. For a small subset of people, lowering the LDL pattern B is more difficult, but adjusting the fat ratio will usually help. (See appendix D for more information.)

When you are in the Keto Zone, your heart, brain, and muscles are also in the zone, for their preferred fuel source is fat rather than sugar. It is good for your entire body. Improved health, renewed energy, incredible clarity, and weight loss—these are just a few of the things you can expect when you are in the Keto Zone.

"Three eggs cooked in grass-fed butter, with a whole avocado, and I am energetic, alert, and full for five hours."
—*Don*

CHAPTER NINE

THE KETO ZONE AND YOUR PROTEIN

The Keto Zone Diet: Low-Carb, High-Fat, **MODERATE-PROTEIN**

ROBBY WAS A MEAT AND POTATOES kind of guy. He had crossed middle age quite gracefully, due in part to his commitment to physical exercise, but he was worried about his numbers.

"It's the creeping game," he joked. "All the bad numbers are slowly creeping up, like my blood pressure, cholesterol, and weight, while all my good numbers are creeping down. The worst, though, are my forty-inch jeans. I used to have a thirty-two-inch waist!"

We discussed foods, carbohydrate sensitivity, insulin resistance, and all that. He was quick to see the importance of losing the belly fat, as it not only annoyed him, it was the probable pathway for disease into his body.

He eased into the Keto Zone diet, wanting to start slowly and build up steam over time. It worked for him, though I explained that most people prefer the jump rather than the slide.

For Robby, cutting out potatoes, grains, and other starches was vital. Replacing those with green veggies and salad veggies took a little getting used to, but he understood the importance of low-carb so he could get into the Keto Zone.

Almost three months later, he checked in. He was all smiles. All the numbers, especially his cholesterol, were going in the right direction. "However, there is one thing," he said. "I just can't seem to squeeze into my thirty-two-inch jeans. I'm stuck, literally. What am I doing wrong?"

After we discussed the three ways to fall out of the Keto Zone (not enough fats, too much protein, or too many carbs), he immediately exclaimed, "It's the protein. I've been eating too much meat and too many whey protein shakes!"

He adjusted, lowering his protein intake quite a bit and increasing his fat intake a little, keeping the green veggies the same. I was impressed that he was keeping his carb intake low for so long, considering his penchant for starches, but getting back into his old clothes was a strong motivation. His usual projects that kept him active were a sufficient exercise program.

About six weeks later, he e-mailed me a short "thanks, doc" and two thumbs-up symbols. It seems those thirty-two-inch jeans were fitting again.

THE POWER OF PROTEIN

Protein is a must for your body. Specifically, you need nine essential amino acids (histidine, isoleucine, leucine, lysine, methionine, phenylalanine, threonine, tryptophan, and valine), and the only way to get them is through the food you eat.

Typical sources include eggs, meat like chicken, turkey, and beef, dairy products, fish, and plant and plant products.

Incidentally, eggs happen to contain every essential amino acid. Combine that with the change in the 2015 US Dietary Guidelines saying it is now healthy to eat the whole egg,[62] and you have a perfect source for protein and amino acids.

Some argue that too much protein, especially from processed meats, increases cancer risks. The International Agency for Research on Cancer, which is an agency of the World Health Organization, classified processed meats as a carcinogen or cancer-causing substance and classified red meat as a probable carcinogen.[63]

From my experience with cancer patients, processed meats like pepperoni, ham, hotdogs, bologna, sausage, salami, and even bacon do not help in the healing process and may even cause cancer. Grass-fed meats, on the other hand, get far better results, so I recommend steering clear of processed meats as much as possible. Eating some in moderation, or rotating them every three to four days, is probably not going to cause you any problems.

> **IT'S A FACT**
>
> Eggs are the best brain food.

Processed meat has been smoked, salted, or cured. It usually contains chemicals such as nitrites that produce N-nitroso compounds that increase the risk of cancer. Eating processed meats and the excessive intake of red meat may increase the risk of colorectal cancer, pancreatic cancer, and prostate cancer.

How much processed meat is too much? One hot dog or four pieces of bacon is enough to increase your risk. If you enjoy processed meats, simply reduce your intake to only two to three pieces of nitrite-free bacon every three to four days, and I recommend consuming a tablespoon of fiber (such as chia seeds) after eating processed meats with 8 ounces of water.

For my advanced cancer patients, I allow 3 to 4 ounces of grass-fed meat twice a week. However, people who do not have cancer can have red meat more often, a serving or two every two to three days.

Proteins are an integral part of the Keto Zone diet. This being a moderate-protein diet, that means there are some limits on protein consumption.

You may be wondering, *Why are there limits on protein if protein is healthy?*

Or maybe you are thinking about it from the weight-loss perspective: *Why are there limits on protein if protein does not have any carbs?*

These are good questions. The Keto Zone limits protein intake because if you eat too much of it, all fat burning usually stops. It is not a matter of healthy proteins or carbohydrates. Rather, it is the fact that too much protein may bump you out of the Keto Zone.

At the cellular level, when you eat more protein than your body can burn or use, the excess is converted by the liver into glucose, almost as if you had eaten sugars or carbs. Your insulin level then goes up, and that throws you out of the Keto Zone. The process is called *gluconeogenesis*. Basically, your body makes its own carbs from the extra proteins you ate.

That is why eating too much protein actually can make you hungrier. The extra proteins are usually converted into sugars, which puts you back into the using-sugar-as-fuel scenario, and fat burning grinds to a stop.

The ideal protein intake ratio for the Keto Zone diet is approximately 1 gram of protein per 1 kilogram (2.2 pounds) of weight.

That breaks down to be about 20 to 30 grams of protein per meal, with 60 to 140 grams as the maximum amount for a day. So someone weighing 180 pounds needs about 80 grams of protein a day, or 27 grams per meal. At 125, 150, or 250 pounds, that is 19, 23, or 38 grams respectively per meal.

To put it another way, with each ounce of protein (egg, fish, chicken, or steak) being about 7 grams of protein, men should eat about 3 to 6 ounces of protein two to three times a day, and women should eat about 3 to 4 ounces of protein two to three times a day. This will help keep you from feeling hungry and usually keep you in the Keto Zone.

You get the picture. And the healthy menus and recipes of the Keto Zone diet make the selection of proteins a very easy process.

Most people get about 30 percent of their total daily calories from the proteins they eat. The Keto Zone diet lowers your protein intake to about 15 percent of your total day's calories. Some may even need to lower it to around 10 percent, but the Keto Zone diet is flexible to meet your needs. (See appendix C for more information for cancer patients.)

Interestingly, if you are sensitive to carbohydrates, it is likely that you are sensitive to excessive proteins as well. As a result, you may need to adjust and lower your protein intake a bit so that you remain in the Keto Zone.

This is what was happening with Robby. He kept slipping in and out of the Keto Zone, and that was not sufficient to burn off his stubborn belly fat. Once he lowered his protein intake, the fat he wanted to lose melted away. He was also less hungry as a result of his small tweaks (less protein, more fat), and he shifted into the Keto Zone.

> **IT'S A FACT**
>
> One egg or an ounce of fish, chicken, or steak, all have about 7 grams of protein.

WHAT COMES WITH THE PROTEIN?

Usually the biggest challenge with protein is what comes with it. With meat, it might be a sugary sauce or a condiment, like ketchup, or a customary side dish, like potatoes with the roast beef, that keeps you out of the Keto Zone.

When it comes to dairy, which can be a great source of protein, it is often hard to recognize just how much sugar and carbs come with the proteins. Most cheeses, especially hard cheeses, include 1 gram of carb per ounce, which makes a slice of cheese easy to count. Just 2 tablespoons (1 fluid ounce) of whole milk has 1.5 grams of carbs.

> ### IT'S A FACT
>
> Eating too much protein will make you hungry just as eating too many carbs will.

Yogurt is an example of where we can get in trouble. It has good bacteria, fermentation, calcium, and protein, but 8 ounces of plain whole-milk yogurt has 10 grams of carbs. Not bad, but if it is low-fat, it is suddenly 43 grams of carbs. If you do two-thirds yogurt with one-third fruit, the 8 ounces of plain whole-milk yogurt now has 20 grams of carbs. If you choose granola instead of fruit, it becomes 30 grams of carbs.

You get the picture. It is easy to see how something presumed healthy, such as a yogurt with fruit, can bump you right out of the Keto Zone.

Beans, such as pinto, black, white, kidney, and red, peas, lentils, and soybeans, may be good sources of protein, but they are notorious for kicking you out of the Keto Zone. A single cup of pinto beans has 32 grams of carbs. That would end your fat-burning plans for the entire day.

With proteins, the unexpected sugars and carbs that come with them need to be taken into account. You may need to swap your favorite source of protein for another one so that you can stay in the Keto Zone. You will know as you go, but just keep that in mind.

If you find that dairy causes problems, such as nasal drainage, sinus congestion, joint aches, dark circles under the eyes, mental sluggishness, bloating, gas, diarrhea, or even flu-like symptoms, then it would be wise to cut back on your dairy intake. These symptoms may be a result of an intolerance, allergy, sensitivity, or inflammation caused by your body's reaction to the casein, whey, lactose, or mold in the dairy. Cheese, for example, contains a lot of mold, and people who are mold sensitive (about 20 to 25 percent of us) may get the same reaction from cheese as they would from mold spores in the air. For that matter, coffee, chocolate, many nuts, grains, most corn, mushy berries, peanuts, and wine often have mold toxins. It is something to consider.

Another concern with protein comes from the manufacturing process. For example, pasteurization briefly heats milk to just over 160 degrees Fahrenheit to kill bad bacteria. The process also kills good bacteria or probiotics, denatures milk proteins, and makes the sugars more rapidly absorbed, which renders pasteurized milk less nutritious than it is in its raw form. Understandably, raw milk brings with it questions of sanitation and possible pathogenic bacteria, viruses, and parasites. (Raw milk kefir or raw milk yogurt are good options, as the fermentation process usually kills the bad bacteria, viruses, and parasites.)

Clearly, a lot of unknowns can accompany protein.

While in the Keto Zone, with fat burning as the goal, the carbohydrate max of 20 grams per day is going to automatically minimize some dairy products. I don't recommend removing dairy completely; instead, just reduce the serving size or eat it only every three to four days so you can remain in the Keto Zone. Also, choose organic and grass-fed dairy if available for butter, ghee, and cheese.

Personally, I eat organic dairy in the form of cheese (in a Caprese salad with mozzarella cheese) every three to four days and look forward to it. But if I eat cheese daily, I get nasal and sinus congestion, excessive mucous production, and dark circles under my eyes.

Dairy is not the only source of protein that comes with other nondesirable elements. As we have discussed, meats often include toxins as a result of what the animals have been fed. It's only logical that animals that are fed nutritiously will produce more nutritious meat.

A cow's stomach is like a four-stage washing machine. With cows, sheep, and goats, grass is ideal. Feeding the animals grains causes them to get bloat, which then requires treatment with antibiotics. The antibiotics in the feed naturally end up in the meat, which we then eat.[64]

Dave Asprey, author of *The Bulletproof Diet*, says it best: "Feeding cattle junk food turns them into junk food. Ruminant animals are meant to eat grass, not grains, stale bread, cereal, chicken feathers, or city garbage, as are sometimes added to cut the cost of animal feed."[65]

The grass-fed meats have more nutrients, omega-3, fats, and trace minerals, which is ideal protein for both weight loss and brain function, not to mention in small amounts it is usually a safe meat protein for cancer patients. Grass-fed meats also contain CLA, a saturated fat found mainly in grass-fed meats, which helps prevent cancer.

We have known for years that the fatty composition in beef that is fed grass versus grain is different. The grass fed has more yellow fat, which is better. The grass-fed meat has more monounsaturated fats, CLA saturated fats, and omega-3 fats, all of them healthier fats.[66] At the supermarket, if you can afford it, get grass-fed meat. You are eating small portions of protein anyway, so if you can, go with grass-fed. Fattier cuts are fine. If you are eating out or do not want to pay for grass-fed, go with grain-fed, and choose the leaner cuts, such as a fillet.

What comes with the protein? That is always a good question to keep in mind. Make sure it is more of what you want, and make sure it helps you stay right in the middle of the Keto Zone.

DETOX AS NEEDED

The Keto Zone is not only the best weight-loss program in the world, it is also an incredible detox for those who want to use it for that. It effectively cleans toxic fats out of your system, flushes out the liver and gallbladder, and goes a long way in protecting your blood vessels from plaque buildup.

Detoxing as needed, and using the Keto Zone diet for weight loss, will be very healthy for your gallbladder and for clearing up a fatty liver.

Interestingly, those who have eaten strictly vegetarian food or even been on low-fat diets may have gallbladder issues without realizing it. The gallbladder helps break down fats after a meal, taking cholesterol through the liver into the bile found in the gallbladder and then finally out through the intestinal tract. But on a low-fat diet or a vegetarian diet, the gallbladder basically collects bile and usually does not release it effectively. That is because dietary fat triggers the hormone cholecystokinin that signals the gallbladder to contract and release bile into the intestines to help you digest fats.

A low-fat diet causes the gallbladder to get lazy. As the bile sits in the gallbladder, the cholesterol and bile form a sludge that can eventually become gallstones.

Adding fat to your diet slowly may be necessary to clear the gallbladder of any accumulated sludge. If you eat fats, such as olive oil with your salad, and feel pain in the right upper quadrant that radiates around to the back or up to the shoulder blade, it may be your gallbladder acting up.

Increasing good fats, as is the case on the Keto Zone diet, will usually help flush out the gallbladder. I often suggest 1 to 2 tablespoons of olive oil two to three times a day to get bile flowing. For some, I recommend only 1 teaspoon of olive oil every hour for eight hours to gently flush out the gallbladder. There are other types of gallbladder flushes, but first see your physician for a gallbladder ultrasound.

IT'S A FACT

"I'm starving!" If you feel that way, you need to increase your intake of fats.

Even a little healthy monounsaturated fats (e.g., olive oil and avocado oil) will typically stop gall-stone formation. (If the pain persists, you may have gall-stones and may need surgery. You will need to see your physician to have the necessary tests.) Feeding your gallbladder the right fats (mainly monounsaturated) will usually flush it out and restore its function again. If your gallbladder does have issues, the Keto Zone will usually reveal it to you, and may help it heal at the same time.

Trans fats, fried foods, and excessive saturated fats can increase one's risk for gallstones. Adequate fiber intake and adequate monounsaturated fats usually prevent gallstones, which is why I recommend that at least half of your fats on the Keto Zone diet should be monounsaturated.

MODERATE PROTEIN IS IDEAL

The fact that the Keto Zone diet is moderate-protein is part of what makes it unique among other ketogenic diets. Not only does protein intake need to be low enough to avoid gluconeogenesis (where your body turns excess proteins into sugar), it also needs to be high enough to provide your body with the essential amino acids that it needs.

This is a delicate balance, one that the Keto Zone diet is able to provide for your body.

In addition, the Keto Zone diet goes a step further with healthy sources of protein and healthy sources of fat from plants and grass-fed animals. This is ideal for fat burning as well as ideal for long-term health.

"I feel great.
No sugar or carb is worth
getting me out of the Keto Zone."
—*Mary*

CHAPTER TEN

THE KETO ZONE AND YOUR APPETITE HORMONES

AS A TEENAGER, BRADDOCK knew he was in trouble. "My parents took us out to eat several times a week because everyone was so busy," he explained. "Pizza and soda were the norm after games or Chinese food to celebrate a special achievement."

In relation to statistics that show we get a third of our daily calories on average from restaurants,[67] Braddock and his family were on the low side of the trend.

Braddock had no complaints about the food. But after leaving high school at a lean and mean 160 pounds, it was not long before he crossed 200. At 240 pounds, he began to have backaches, pains in his joints, and high blood pressure. His doctor strongly suggested he start taking cholesterol-lowering drugs right away.

"I know what my ideal weight should be, and I know the food I eat is not all that healthy. All that makes sense to me," he said. "But what I do not understand is how I can still be hungry after I eat a big meal."

"Why do you wonder about that?" I asked him. I was curious what his logic was and hoped it would help him find his answers.

His answer was very insightful. "If I can eat and still be hungry, then what is going to stop me from eating even more?" he said. "I'm only thirty years old, and I'm already obese. What's going to prevent me from dying of diabetes, heart disease, or some other disease at an early age?"

He was scared. I could see it. But it was a healthy type of fear. He wanted an answer that he could live with, as it would no doubt affect everything about him.

When I explained how the appetite hormones ghrelin and leptin are often out of sync in people who need to lose weight, he chuckled. "That's me. The 'I'm full' signal never gets to my head."

He was exactly right. When appetite hormone levels are messed up, the signals "I'm full" or "I'm satisfied" usually don't reach the brain on time, and that translates directly into more weight gain.

Braddock was right to be afraid. Thankfully, he took action and changed things before it was too late.

HOW YOUR HORMONES SABOTAGE YOU

For many years we have known there to be two key appetite hormones, leptin (decreases our hunger) and ghrelin (increases our hunger). Usually when we have not eaten for at least three or four hours, ghrelin levels are high and unleash a ravenous appetite. Leptin is a little more complicated and will be discussed. These hormones turn on or turn off usually based on the food we eat.

What gets problematic and discouraging is that as we age, become obese, or eat foods containing certain food additives (such as MSG), our bodies fail to properly read or interpret correctly our own appetite hormones.

As a result, what should have been simple is not. Ideally, when we eat a meal and our body produces more leptin that says, "Okay, you are full, stop eating," we stop. That's the normal process.

In addition, since leptin is produced in our fatty tissue, the more fat we have, the more leptin we should make. Obese people usually have more leptin, and in theory their leptin levels should be yelling, "You're full. Stop eating!" And because they're full, they should stop eating, lose weight, and burn off the fat. But just because it *should* does not mean it *will*.

What actually happens is that the brain and body fail to communicate due to leptin resistance. This is part and parcel of carbohydrate sensitivity. As a result, the body not only misses the signal for feeling full and there is no decrease in appetite, but the person may actually feel hungrier than ever, which only compounds the problem. That was precisely what Braddock recognized. He saw it, but did not know what to do about it.

> ### IT'S A FACT
> Fructose, which is the sugar in fruit and fruit juices, helps increase leptin resistance.[68]

There is no magic leptin pill, shot, or supplement. Researchers have tried that approach, and it did not work. To get leptin to work properly, there is no real shortcut.

Ghrelin, on the other hand, is the hormone that tells us we are hungry. It is made in the stomach and intestines, so if your stomach feels empty, you naturally feel hungry. Your appetite increases. That is ghrelin hard at work.

You have more ghrelin in your body when you are hungry and less after you have eaten. On a practical level, if you forget to eat a meal or purposefully skip a meal, maybe trying to lose weight, your body pumps out more ghrelin, thus the "I'm starving" feeling.

While keeping ghrelin levels low is supposed to help manage our body weight, the task is almost impossible if we are eating a low-fat diet. Ghrelin levels decrease for about three to four hours after a meal and then begin to rise. Having sufficient fat in the diet is helpful because it delays gastric emptying and lowers ghrelin levels for many more hours, which suppresses appetite significantly.

High ghrelin levels (due to a low-fat diet) create a downward spiral that does not stop. The results are what we see around us in society with the epidemics of obesity, diabetes, high blood pressure, heart disease, and much more.

Conversely, and logically, the less body fat we have, the better our leptin works to turn off our appetite, which in turn helps us manage our weight and metabolism.

It is next to impossible to lose weight when your own appetite hormones are sabotaging you. If these hormones are out of balance, the usual "eat less food and exercise more" advice will probably re-sult in more weight gain.

Some people try low-calorie diets, but eating less than 1,000 calories a day will eventually lead to high ghrelin levels and uncon-trollable hunger. When we do not consume adequate calories or ad-equate dietary fat, ghrelin levels rise, and we may become hungrier, even "hangry" (hungry and angry). After all, it is low calories and high ghrelin, so it only makes sense to be starving. Sadly, that is the exact reason why weight gain after going on a diet is so common.

This yo-yo effect is something that many people come to despise.

But if there were a way to bring the appetite hormones into bal-ance, a way to make ghrelin and leptin hormones function as they are supposed to, would that not be a huge breakthrough for every-one trying to lose weight, especially those battling obesity?

It would, indeed, be huge news! It could change—and save—

millions of lives each year. It would probably reverse obesity rates, shave billions off our expenses, and keep untold numbers of people out of the hospital.

You know by now that there is a way to bring this much-needed balance to our appetite hormones. It is the Keto Zone diet. And once you hit the Keto Zone, your appetite hormones are usually completely balanced. You are the one who is in control.

Beautifully, the appetite hormones cannot sabotage your weight-loss plans when you are the one in control.

BALANCE IS VITAL

The greatest hormone balance we need in our bodies is the balance of leptin and ghrelin. When those two hormones are balanced, we usually have appetite control.

Imagine losing weight and not being hungry. Most often, that is precisely what happens on the Keto Zone diet. Your hunger is usually controlled because your ghrelin and leptin levels eventually are under control.

Technically, you will feel "full" and "satisfied" on two different levels at the same time. The high-fat and moderate-protein foods and veggies will do that for you, but there is an internal feeling of satisfaction taking place as well. Your ketones, which are around 0.1 millimolar in the morning (normal for most people who have not eaten anything since dinner), will rise as a result of what you are eating on your Keto Zone diet. Ketone levels of 0.5 millimolar will suppress your appetite.[69]

This means the food and the ketones are working in your favor to control your appetite hormones, and that makes you the one in control of your appetite.

It is the ideal spot for weight loss. As Jimmy Moore and Dr. Eric

Westman wrote in *Keto Clarity*, "When you start to burn fat for fuel and produce ketones, it's very possible to feel completely satisfied and energized on one, maybe two meals a day."[70]

Here are a few more benefits of finding balance in the Keto Zone:

- The increase in your omega-3 fat intake on the Keto Zone diet boosts your leptin and helps reverse leptin resistance. This decreases hunger.[71]
- Ghrelin levels do not typically go up when your body is in the Keto Zone because ketosis suppresses the ghrelin levels that usually occur with weight loss.[72]
- The Keto Zone is low-carb, but the fats and proteins help balance your appetite hormones, and you usually have a full or satisfied feeling without food cravings. Most carbs such as potatoes, rice, and pasta may spend only thirty minutes in your stomach and may take only two hours to digest and absorb fully. Proteins take longer to digest than carbs, but fats take the most time to digest and absorb, helping to lower ghrelin levels.

One aspect of balancing appetite hormones that surprises many people is the integral part that sleep plays in the overall process. In fact, sleep is a vital part of balancing the appetite hormones and weight loss.

Somewhere between six and eight hours of sleep is ideal. Insufficient sleep makes your body produce less leptin and more ghrelin.[73]

Lack of sleep also messes with your glucose and insulin levels, and as you know, controlling those levels is vital to weight loss and appetite control.[74]

In the Keto Zone, you will find that your body may actually need less sleep. Some people function incredibly well with four to five hours, but six and a half hours is a common amount of sleep that produces rest, comfort, and health. If you need a full eight hours of sleep now, that is fine. Just do not be surprised if that number eventually goes down over time in the Keto Zone.

Getting your ghrelin and leptin hormones to function properly is an absolute necessity to any weight-loss program, and it will usually happen as you continue on the Keto Zone diet. The longer you stay in the Keto Zone, the easier it becomes and the more control you have over your appetite hormones.

Staying in the Keto Zone or in nutritional ketosis means you are burning mainly fats for energy. This in turn prevents spikes in insulin and major fluctuations in blood sugar that would also trigger hunger.

> ### IT'S A FACT
>
> Get your sleep and get in the Keto Zone—that is how you balance appetite hormones.

ADDITIVES THAT ACTUALLY SUBTRACT

Weight loss is all about appetite control. If you can control your appetite, you can usually control your weight and weight loss.

That is one of the strengths of the Keto Zone diet because through it you are the one in control of your appetite. The grehlin and leptin appetite hormones, in essence, work for you and help you accomplish your weight-loss goals.

Naturally, you are going to face resistance. Here are three of the biggest food additives that are roadblocks to your appetite control.

MSG

A food additive that makes foods taste better, MSG (monosodium glutamate) blocks messages to your brain that you are full, which simply means you keep eating, and that, in turn, can eventually cause leptin resistance. Specifically, MSG increases insulin levels, and the surge of insulin causes your blood sugar to plummet and your hunger to spike. You are hungry all over again! MSG can triple the amount of insulin released by the pancreas. Research has shown that MSG can increase the appetite of rats by up to 40 percent.[75]

As you would expect, MSG is almost everywhere, including most processed foods, crackers, chips, salty snacks, soups, frozen meals, deli meats, gravies, Asian foods, and fast foods.

Spotting MSG on the label is not that easy because it is often hidden under another name, such as:

glutamate

calcium caseinate

autolyzed yeast extract

hydrolyzed protein

hydrolyzed vegetable protein

hydrolyzed plant protein

yeast extract

plant protein extract

textured protein

hydrolyzed oat flour

sodium caseinate

monopotassium glutamate

glutamic acid

gelatin

Ajinomoto[76]

ARTIFICIAL SWEETENERS

Right up there with MSG is another additive that really messes with your hormones and neurotransmitters. It also is known by many names, but at its core it is an artificial sweetener.

Artificial sweeteners, such as aspartame, sucralose, saccharine, and acesulfame potassium, are often recommended for weight loss. Recent research from the University of Sydney has found that artificial sweeteners can increase calorie consumption by up to 30 percent. In the study, fruit flies were exposed to a diet high in artificial sweeteners for a prolonged period of time (five days). Researchers found that the artificial sweeteners caused an increased appetite, and 30 percent more calories were consumed. When they were given food that was naturally sweetened, "we found that inside the brain's reward centers, sweet sensation is integrated with energy content. When sweeteners versus energy is out of balance for a period of time, the brain recalibrates and increases total calories consumed," according to the lead researcher, associate professor Gregory Neely.

> ### IT'S A FACT
> Sweet beverages, including fruit juices, raise your leptin numbers, which only makes you hungrier.

Neely went on to say, "When we investigated why animals were eating more even though they had enough calories, we found that chronic consumption of this artificial sweetener actually increases the sweet intensity of real nutritive sugar and this then increases the animal's overall motivation to eat more food."[77]

Put another way, when regular sugar is consumed, the pleasure-reward neurotransmitter dopamine is released from the brain, and sugar levels rise in the bloodstream. However, when artificial sweeteners are consumed, dopamine is also released, but the blood sugar does not rise. The brain then sends hunger signals requesting more food.

Artificial sweeteners have so many negative side effects that they should never be seen as a "zero" calorie option.

Healthy sweeteners for beverages or cooking that will still keep you in the Keto Zone include stevia, erythritol, xylitol (go light with xylitol because too much can cause gastrointestinal upset), and monk fruit (lo han guo).

HFCS

A more common name for HFCS that sounds "safe" is high fructose corn syrup. It is a chemical creation that transforms glucose into fructose. It is made from natural ingredients, but it is very man-made, even acting as a preservative in foods. It is quite inexpensive to create, which is why it accounts for about half of the sweeteners eaten today.[78]

Just like MSG and artificial sweeteners, high fructose corn syrup is almost everywhere, including most sweets, canned fruits and veggies, sodas, yogurts, peanut butter, ketchup, frozen meals, pasta, baked goods, cookies, and much more. Most likely, almost every single processed food item in the fridge contains some high fructose corn syrup.

Not surprisingly, it plays a direct role in the obesity and diabetes epidemics. When you eat it:

- Blood sugar levels rise
- Insulin levels rise
- The liver converts the fructose quickly and directly into fat

With that type of reaction, it should be no surprise that high fructose corn syrup is linked to belly fat, dementia, gout, high triglycerides, fatty liver, high cholesterol, and heart disease.

Supposing that HFCS is in almost everything we eat, and we eat every three to four hours (meals and snacks), not to mention beverages sweetened with HFCS that we drink all day long, then it would be pretty safe to assume we are having insulin spikes, weight gain, and fat storage all day long. Yes, that is the norm, and with it comes hunger pains an hour or two after we eat or drink a beverage containing HFCS.

To further mess with your hormones, sugar triggers a release of dopamine in your brain. Dopamine is the motivation neurotransmitter and is in charge of your pleasure-reward system. It allows you to have feelings of enjoyment, bliss, and euphoria. It boosts your drive, focus, and concentration.

With every high comes a low, and that means you usually need more sugar to get the same feeling you had before. Sugar cravings are natural, you "need" to have more, and usually your body is saying, "Right now!"

Many people have low dopamine levels and with it low energy and motivation. High fructose corn syrup in countless foods offers a temporary dopamine boost that helps them get through the day.

This high and low and constant intake of sweets, which usually goes straight to stored fat, is stopped by the Keto Zone diet. As for healthier ways to boost your dopamine, low-sugar dark chocolate (more than 85 percent

> **IT'S A FACT**
>
> If you don't control your appetite, you won't lose weight.

cocoa), green tea, or curry will help, but the Keto Zone diet is very effective in balancing the need for food. That is the biggest yo-yo ride that comes to an end.

These three, high fructose corn syrup, MSG, and artificial sweeteners, are additives that do not add anything of value to your body.

They will sabotage your weight loss, create food cravings, imbalance your appetite hormones, cause insulin spikes, and program you for obesity and a host of other diseases. They eventually bankrupt your body and give you nothing in return.

KEEP THE GOAL IN MIND

Appetite hormones may kick and scream, but eventually they will obey you and come into balance. They have no choice because they only have as much power as you give them, and food is power.

Those overpowering feelings of intense hunger, a sign that ghrelin levels are elevated and you are leptin resistant, will have no choice but to subside and go away. Eating healthy foods that are high-fat and moderate-protein with lots of veggies will remove hunger problems and usually balance appetite hormones and reverse leptin resistance.

The goal is weight loss, and with the Keto Zone diet, you can put the appetite hormones in their proper place. Appetite hormones, after all, are here to serve you. This is what usually happens as a result of a few short days and weeks on the Keto Zone diet:

$$\text{controlled hormones} = \text{controlled appetite} = \text{weight loss!}$$

If appetite hormones are not brought under control and balanced, the end result is weight gain and with it many of the preventable diseases that plague the world today.

Yes, weight loss is a goal worth fighting for, but is it *the* goal? Is it the biggest goal you are chasing?

Maybe you want to wear that expensive dress again? Or fit into those jeans? Or stop covering up? Or run that 5K race with your children? Or hike that mountain? Or buy that motorcycle? Or go on that cruise? Or get your health back?

There are countless reasons for losing weight, but the big goals, the ones that touch your inner heart strings, such as being able to play with your children and grandchildren or dance with your son or daughter at their wedding, will motivate you to take action, regardless of what anyone else might say, think, or do.

Keep that true goal of yours in mind as you dive into the Keto Zone diet.

IT'S A FACT

Green veggies and salad veggies also help to curb hunger because they are usually high in water and fiber and low in carbs. If they are eaten in sufficient amounts with meals, they will add bulk to your meal, filling your stomach and helping you feel full and satisfied.

PART THREE

How to Put the Keto Zone Diet to Work for You

Simple steps to implement the Keto Zone diet and exactly what it takes to get you into the fat-burning zone as well as practical shopping guides, step-by-step instructions, and menu plans.

You have come a long way. Having read the first ten chapters, you know more about how the body functions than most people. You also know exactly why getting in the Keto Zone is so effective for weight loss. That is where we are going. To get there, it is simply a matter of following the steps.

CHAPTER ELEVEN

PUTTING YOUR PLAN INTO ACTION

TONY LOVED HIS BEER. Drinking close to a dozen a day, it was no surprise that he developed a beer gut.

What surprised him, though, was a diagnosis of diabetes. His doctor told him, "You are on your way to dialysis or a massive heart attack or going blind or an amputation if you don't lay off the beer."

Tony was already having circulation trouble in his legs, and when his doctor told him that if his diabetes remained untreated it could eventually lead to the amputation of his feet, Tony exclaimed, "That's it, I'm off alcohol. Nothing is worth that." He took immediate action. Out went the beer, and within four months he had lost forty pounds. His sugar levels even returned to normal.

An amputation was not a concern any longer. Imagining himself in a wheelchair with no feet stirred Tony to action. He was an avid sports fan who played basketball, baseball, and softball and was always going to sports games, and nothing was worth giving that up!

Tony had his light-bulb moment, and he woke up before it was too late. Any alcohol can sabotage your weight loss and will prevent you from entering the Ketzo Zone.

THE PLAN LAID OUT

You already know how and why the Keto Zone diet is the healthiest, fastest, and easiest way to lose weight. Now it is time to put that knowledge into action.

The best place to begin is with the big picture of what it takes to implement the Keto Zone diet. It looks like this:

1. Know where you are aiming
2. Go shopping for the right ingredients
3. Get in the Keto Zone
4. Stay in the Keto Zone with the right menu plans
5. Discover your KCL number to maintain your ideal weight

It really is not complicated at all.

KNOW WHERE YOU ARE AIMING

The food you eat is your answer to weight loss and good health, and that is where the Keto Zone diet begins. To review, the foods that make up the Keto Zone diet break down into this format:

FATS: 70 percent of daily caloric intake from healthy fats including fish oil, healthy monounsaturated fats, healthy saturated fats, and minimal healthy polyunsaturated fats.

PROTEINS: Approximately 15 percent of daily caloric intake from healthy protein including pastured eggs, wild fish, grass-fed meats, nuts, and some dairy.

CARBS: Approximately 15 percent of daily caloric intake from salad veggies, nonstarchy veggies, green veggies, spices, and herbs.

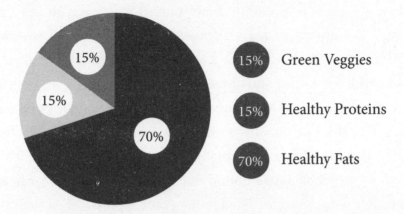

When you are consuming this ratio of foods, your body cannot help but shift into fat-burning mode. It is the "sweet spot," the Keto Zone, where you have a lot of energy, your appetite hormones are balanced, and fat is melting off at a rate of about one to three pounds per week.

That is where you are aiming (see chapter 12).

GO SHOPPING FOR THE RIGHT INGREDIENTS

Thankfully, you do not need to count calories. But you do need to restock your shelves. Invade your pantry, fridge, and freezer, and get rid of the unhealthy, tempting foods that will bump you out of the Keto Zone.

To make things easy, there is a specific list of proteins, fats, and green veggie carbs that you can get to restock your shelves (see chapter 13). There are many great foods to choose from, so you can restock as you see fit. Just make sure it keeps you in the Keto Zone (see chapter 13).

GET IN THE KETO ZONE

When you are in the Keto Zone, typically you are burning fat without hunger or food cravings, your appetite hormones usually are balanced, and you ordinarily find yourself with vast amounts of energy. You are often sharp, engaged, and full of life, all without increased appetite, food cravings, weight gain, or counting calories.

In addition to the usual four to five pounds of weight loss the first week, you may burn as much as one to two pounds of fat per week after that. Throw in brisk exercise and the Keto Zone coffee for breakfast, and you can usually expect to lose three pounds a week. Some people lose a pound of fat per day! That is great news for people who are accustomed to the exact opposite when they are hoping to lose weight.

The transitioning process from sugar-burning to fat-burning is usually smooth, but if you get caught in the middle, flu-like symptoms can develop. Thankfully, there are ways to avoid this entirely or get past it quickly (see chapter 14).

STAY IN THE KETO ZONE WITH THE RIGHT MENU PLANS

Staying in the Keto Zone is incredibly easy. It is so simple that you will not even need to measure your carbs. Follow the meal plans, and you will be right where you want to be, right in the middle of the fat-burning Keto Zone (see chapter 15).

DISCOVER YOUR KCL NUMBER TO MAINTAIN YOUR IDEAL WEIGHT

The KCL (Keto Carb Limit) number is the line in the sand that defines the effectiveness of all weight-loss efforts. By learning what your KCL number is, you know exactly how many carbs you can eat to continue to lose weight and how many carbs you can eat to maintain your weight or to start gaining weight again.

When you know your KCL number, the tables turn. You are the one in charge. You have the power. There is no longer an unseen force to disrupt your weight-loss plans. All of that is past.

After you have been in the Keto Zone for four to eight weeks and have lost a significant amount of weight, you may be ready to find your KCL number. The process is simple and easy.

With your KCL number in hand, life takes on a whole new meaning. Weight loss is no longer scary or intimidating. From that point forward, everything is better (see chapter 16).

KEEP YOUR "WHY" HANDY

It is always wise and healthy to keep your reason for going on the Keto Zone diet handy. Some patients have told me, "I'm going to get on the Keto Zone diet, lose weight, and then get on it later for detox or to lose weight again if I need to."

That is great. Using the Keto Zone as a detox program, weight-loss program, or both makes great sense.

Some want specifically to improve or reverse their type 2 diabetes. Others want to lessen neurological disease.

On the general health level, some people are pleased to find out that being on a ketogenic diet means they are much less susceptible to viruses and bacterial infections.[79]

For me, I remember my father and am thankful that ketogenic diets have great potential to both prevent and sometimes reverse Alzheimer's.[80]

For you, your motivating "why" may be specifically weight loss, health-related, or even future-focused. Whatever it is that moves you to take action, keep it fresh and in front of you as you dive into the amazing Keto Zone diet.

"I lost 75 pounds.
It's actually easy to do
once you believe,
and know you can do it."
—*Angela*

CHAPTER TWELVE

KNOW WHERE
YOU ARE AIMING

THE WEDDING WAS EIGHT WEEKS AWAY, and Susan was determined to fit into that dress. It was not quite a glass-slipper moment (where Cinderella's stepsisters went to great lengths to fit into the glass slipper), but it felt like it.

Though being a bridesmaid was not quite as stressful as being the bride, Susan was still going to be front and center, and pictures of the wedding would last a lifetime.

During those eight weeks, the plan was simple: starve. That is what Susan did. Headaches, mood swings, and food cravings were the daily norm, but she persisted. Come hell or high water—"or death," her husband now jokes—Susan was going to fit into her dress.

In the end, she felt sick and tired, gaunt and depressed, but she was able to squeeze into the dress. Though she was not 100 percent pleased with how she looked in the photos, she felt satisfied that she got into her dress. Mission accomplished!

The weeks that followed the wedding went by quickly. She felt better because she was eating again, but she wondered what would happen to her weight. Within a few months, as she half expected, she had surpassed her previous weight.

"Living by starving is no way to live life at all," she said as she sat in my office. "Surely there is a way to lose weight that doesn't kill me in the process."

I assured her there was. As you know, it is called the Keto Zone diet.

EXPECTATIONS AT THE START

When you start the Keto Zone diet, you can expect to lose about four pounds the first week as your body dumps its stored sugar and water and then usually one to two pounds of fat every week after that.

If you add in fifteen to thirty minutes of exercise per day (five days a week), you can usually increase the burn rate to two to three pounds of fat loss per week. I have even seen people really ramp up the exercise while on the Keto Zone diet and lose a pound of fat per day. While I do not usually recommend it, I find it encouraging to know it is possible. But for most people, a slow and steady one to three pounds of fat loss per week is my recommendation.

As for expectations, here are several you can look forward to:

- *Food cravings:* You can usually expect not to have food cravings because your insulin levels have been reduced so much that you will no longer be having insulin spikes or the food cravings that come with it.
- *Appetite control:* You can usually expect full appetite control because being in the Keto Zone turns off your appetite.
- *Belly fat:* You can usually expect to burn primarily belly fat.
- *Mental clarity:* You can usually expect to be sharp, focused, and clear headed.

- *Improved energy:* You can usually expect to be full of energy. In the Keto Zone, your body taps into an energy source (burning fats as fuel) that far surpasses your body's previous energy source (burning sugars as fuel). It is almost a limitless fuel supply, so be ready to have more energy than ever.

- *Better numbers all around:* You can usually expect to see your good HDL cholesterol increase, bad LDL cholesterol decrease (specifically LDL pattern B), triglycerides decrease, and blood pressure and blood sugar level decrease. Also, inflammatory markers including CRP (C-reactive protein) usually decrease. And the numbers on the scales? Those go down as well. (I suggest weighing just once per week, not daily. For women, it is common to gain one to two pounds during their period, but it is usually due to fluctuating hormones and fluid retention, which means it is temporary.)

Other expectations while in the Keto Zone usually include feelings of happiness, youthfulness, appetite control for five to eight hours between meals, less anxiety, improved sex drive, faster recovery from strenuous workouts, and much more, all of which are good signs you are in the Keto Zone.

If you are like most people, you are thinking, *Good to know, but how fast can I get into the Keto Zone?*

The short answer: it depends on your body.

Usually, it takes two to five days to get into the Keto Zone and begin to produce minor amounts of ketones (0.5–5 millimolar on the urine test strips) that show your body is in the fat-burning mode. It may take your body as long as one to two weeks. Some of my patients who are very carbohydrate sensitive and insulin resistant, or who have pre-diabetes, type 2 diabetes, or are very overweight have taken almost three weeks to get into the Keto Zone. Rarely, some people need to lower their carb intake to only 10 grams of carbs a day to enter the Keto Zone.

For most people, however, the Keto Zone becomes a reality around day two to five, but rest assured, your body will eventually obey you. Keep eating the foods that get you into the Keto Zone, and eventually you will find yourself right in the center of the Keto Zone. It will happen. Trust me. It is inevitable.

Commonly, people will notice their ketone levels inching up around day two or day three, and by day five they are usually deep into the Keto Zone. You will get there, I promise. And though it is a great feeling when you do reach the Keto Zone, it is far more satisfying and fun when you see the fat melting away.

> ### IT'S A FACT
> You can stay in the fat-burning zone for as long as you want.

As for falling out of the Keto Zone, that can only happen if you do not eat enough fats, eat too much protein, or eat too many carbs. Just keep an eye on your ketone levels and adjust your foods accordingly, but if you stick with the diet, you will stay in the Keto Zone. Worst case, if you happen to fall out of the Keto Zone for one reason or another, whether by accident or on purpose, do not berate yourself or feel bad about it. You are usually only two or three Keto Zone meals (twelve hours) away from reentering the Keto Zone. Remember, after you fast for about twelve hours overnight, typically you'll be in mild ketosis.

The good news is you can stay in the Keto Zone and keep burning fat for as long as you want.

WHAT THE FOOD LOOKS LIKE

The Keto Zone diet at its core is low-carb, high-fat, and moderate-protein. That translates into the ratio of 70 percent fats, 15 percent proteins, and 15 percent green veggie carbs. Now we are going to break the plan down and show you what it looks like in real life.

The Keto Zone diet begins at the very low-carb intake of 20 grams per day. After four to eight weeks, you can raise that carb amount slightly until you find your KCL (Keto Carb Limit) number, the point at which you know exactly what your body needs to stay healthy and not gain weight.

You can, of course, stay at 20 grams of carbs per day for as long as you want to keep burning fat at the steady pace of one to three pounds per week. After you have achieved your ideal weight, then you can increase your carbs until you find your KCL number. From there, you can walk balanced and healthy, without gaining back any of the weight you lost.

You are probably thinking, *What does that look like in the real world?*

Getting started on the Keto Zone diet looks something like this:

MEALS

The three main meals on the Keto Zone diet will, of course, vary, but they often take this shape:

Breakfasts: 2 to 3 eggs with 2 tablespoons of grass-fed butter (or, even better, 1 tablespoon grass-fed butter and 1 tablespoon olive oil) and slices of avocado, or coffee with 1 tablespoon of MCT oil powder or MCT oil and 1 tablespoon of avocado oil.

Lunches: Big salad, with dressing made of three parts extra-virgin olive oil to one part apple cider vinegar (add onion juice, garlic, or blended avocado and other herbs and spices if desired), and a serving of protein, such as tuna salad with eggs, celery, and onion or chicken salad with olive oil or avocado oil mayo.

Dinners: Steamed veggies with 2 tablespoons of butter or olive oil (or 1 tablespoon of each) with a serving of protein, such as steak, shrimp scampi, or wild salmon. Note: Use more olive oil and less butter if you are concerned with high cholesterol (see appendix D).

Every meal includes:

1. Necessary fats (about 2 to 3 tablespoons of good fats per meal for women, about 3 to 4 tablespoons per meal for men)
2. Necessary proteins (3 to 4 ounces of protein for women per meal, 3 to 6 ounces of protein for men per meal)
3. Necessary green veggie carbs (about 2 to 6 cups of salad and 1 to 2 cups of cooked veggies per day)

SNACKS

Snacks such as a handful of nuts, celery with 1 to 2 tablespoons of cream cheese or almond butter, or a single slice of cheese are all good options for midmorning or midafternoon. Snacks are usually not needed once you are in the Keto Zone and may slow down your weight loss.

You want snacks that include good fats and good proteins. Be careful, though, because some nuts (especially peanuts, which are not a nut but a legume, and cashews) have more carbs than others, and too many carbs will bump you out of the Keto Zone, regardless of where the carbs might have come from.

BEVERAGES

You will want to drink about 8 ounces of water several times each day, either before or after meals preferably. This is not a drown-myself-so-I'm-not-hungry type of diet. The fats and the proteins are what hold hunger at bay. Drink water as you need. I recommend alkaline, spring water, or filtered water.

Other beverages include coffee, tea, and a few select nut milks. Be careful with beverage sweeteners. This is where many people knock themselves out of the Keto Zone diet by accident. Use stevia or monk fruit (lo han guo) in powder or liquid form to sweeten coffee and teas. It is also okay to use sweet alcohols such as erythritol and xylitol as sweeteners, but stevia is the cheapest and easiest to find. Steer clear of sugar, agave nectar, liquid syrups, honey, and all artificial sweeteners.

> ### IT'S A FACT
> Fats help your body produce more ketones, and that burns off body fat even faster.

SUPPLEMENTS

Lastly, your food intake on the Keto Zone diet will need to include a multivitamin and a few vitamin supplements. At least half of the US population has an inadequate intake of magnesium (according to NHANES survey, 2005–2006), and most people are low in vitamin D, so a good multivitamin and vitamin D supplement will usually provide your body with the vitamins and minerals you need. (If you're over fifty years of age or post menopausal, choose a multivitamin without iron.)

Approximately 90 percent of the US population has inadequate levels of omega-3 in their blood, but taking fish oil or krill oil capsules takes care of that (see appendix A for more information).

Some people also may need an enzyme supplement with extra lipase, especially if they develop loose stools or diarrhea on the Keto Zone diet. Lipase is the enzyme that digests fats. Many people over age fifty-five cannot produce adequate amounts of pancreatic enzymes, so an enzyme supplement is helpful.

And that is usually it. Yes, there are more specifics in the chapters to come, but this brief breakdown of foods and beverages is a rough framework of what you can expect on the Keto Zone diet.

As for the 20 grams of carbs per day limit, you will not usually cross it if you stick with foods and drinks like the ones outlined above. That means you will be in the Keto Zone, burning fat all day and all night.

And that is a wonderful thing!

READY TO JUMP INTO THE KETO ZONE

Over the years in working with patients who are ready to jump into the Keto Zone to lose weight or combat a sickness, a lot of questions naturally arise. Every question is a good one, but here are many that I have received. I hope they will be the questions you wanted to ask.

Why start with the extreme 20 grams carb limit?
The 20 grams of carbs per day is a limit that will usually be low enough to kick-start healthy nutritional ketosis where the body burns fat for fuel rather than burning sugars. Most people hover around 50 to 75 grams as their ideal KCL (Keto Carb Limit) number, which means 20 grams is low enough to start the fat-burning engines. If we started at 50 grams of carbs and your KCL is 50 grams

of carbs, you would neither gain nor lose weight. This is precisely the point you want to reach eventually, but only after you have achieved your ideal weight.

How long can I stay in the Keto Zone?

Stay as long as you want. When you reach your ideal weight, increase your carb intake little by little until you see you are dropping in and out of ketosis. This is your KCL number. Staying at your KCL number usually means no more weight gain.

How can I max this out?

If you want to shed as much fat as possible, you can lower protein intake to 5 to 10 percent of total calories, boost fats to 80 percent, and lower carbs to 10 percent healthy green veggies. Add in twenty to thirty minutes of high-intensity interval training (bike, treadmill, elliptical, or weight lifting) three to five times a week, and you may be burning one pound of fat each day, especially if you drink Keto Zone coffee instead of eating breakfast. (If you are over forty-five years of age, getting a stress test or EKG before starting high-intensity training would be wise.) If you have not been on a regular exercise program, do not start with high-intensity interval training.

If you want to lose one pound a day, skip breakfast and drink a cup or two of Keto Zone coffee, which is organic, single-sourced coffee (most likely to be mold free) with 1 tablespoon of MCT oil powder or MCT oil and 1 tablespoon of avocado oil or grass-fed butter. (You can add stevia or 1/2 teaspoon of dark cocoa to taste.) It will put you in the Keto Zone, and you will usually not be hungry for three to five hours or longer. Then have a Keto Zone lunch and dinner, and you'll have jump-started your metabolism. I prefer MCT oil powder over MCT oil because too much MCT oil may cause diarrhea, whereas MCT oil powder usually will not. Both forms of MCT oil will put you in the Keto Zone for burning fat. (See appendix A for more information.)

What if I bump myself out of the Keto Zone?
Just get back in. You are usually only a day or less away (around twelve hours) from being back in the fat-burning zone.

What if I keep falling in and out of the Keto Zone?
It would seem that you need to adjust things slightly. My guess is that you are getting too many carbs, but it may also be too much protein or not enough fats. First, look at your carbs and then your proteins. It would not hurt to increase your fat intake slightly and make sure it's a 50/50 mix of saturated and monounsaturated fats.

How do I check my ketone levels?
When you are in the Keto Zone, your ketones will usually register at 0.5 to 3 millimolars, however 0.5 to 5 millimolars is also good. For the first month, use urine test strips to measure your ketone (acetoacetate) levels, but beyond that a ketone breath analyzer (to measure acetone) or a blood ketone monitor (to measure beta-hydroxybutyrate) will do the trick. Either can be found online, but I prefer the ketone breath analyzer, such as the one made by Ketonix.

How do I know if I am in the Keto Zone?
If you are burning fat, have no hunger or cravings, your weight is going down, or you see ketones in your urine (or breathe analyzer or blood ketone monitor), you are in the Keto Zone.

Do I need to count my calories?
No, you should not have to count your calories. Just follow the recommended food options, and you usually will be fine. There are times when you will need to count carbs to make sure you are below the 20-gram threshold per day, but even that may not be required if you stay close to the recommended foods and portion sizes.

What if I get hungry during the day?
If you get hungry during the day, it usually means you are not getting enough fats. Increase your fats with grass-fed butter, oils, nuts, or cheese. (If you are hungry because you bumped yourself out of the Keto Zone, that could be the result of too much carbs or too much protein.) Watch the carbs!

Can I still eat dairy?
If you want dairy, go ahead and eat it (my wife likes jalapeño cream cheese with celery sticks), but it is best to alternate days or use small amounts, about 4 ounces a day. Use full cream (best) or half-and-half, both of which are 1 gram of carb per 2 tablespoons, in your coffee rather than milk. Overall, it is hard to stay in the Keto Zone and under 20 grams of carbs if you eat excessive dairy. Also, many of my patients are either sensitive or allergic to dairy, so it usually works best not to eat dairy every day but to alternate dairy every two to four days. Whenever I eat

> **IT'S A FACT**
>
> A study of 42 European countries over a period of 16 years found that eating cereals, wheat, and potatoes increased the risk of heart disease. Dairy was not the cause.[81]

cheese or butter, I usually balance it with equal amounts of either olive oil or avocado oil, which keeps my HDL high and my LDL low. (See appendix D for more information.)

Can I still eat chocolate?

Absolutely! In fact, I recommend it. Dark (85 percent cacao) low-sugar chocolate or dark chocolate with stevia instead of sugar a couple times a day boosts dopamine levels, which give you happy feelings, help turn off food cravings, and improve blood flow to the brain. Enjoy a couple of squares once or twice a day. Dark chocolate contains mainly the saturated fat stearate that raises the good HDL cholesterol and has no effect on the bad LDL cholesterol. I usually enjoy two small squares of dark chocolate every evening for my dessert.

How much protein are we talking about?

Protein intake should be about 1 gram per 1 kilogram (2.2 pounds) of body weight:

- 250 pounds—113 grams, or about 38 grams per meal
- 180 pounds—80 grams, or about 27 grams per meal
- 150 pounds—70 grams, or about 23 grams per meal

On your plate, that is approximately 3 to 4 ounces of protein two to three times a day for women and 3 to 6 ounces of protein two to three times a day for men. One ounce of protein (egg, fish, chicken, or steak) is typically 7 grams of protein. This amount will help to keep you from feeling hungry and usually keep you in the Keto Zone. Too much protein and your body will start to convert the excess protein to glucose, and you will be out of the Keto Zone.

Can I eat any bread at all?

Apart from a few specialty breads, such as seed bread, which boasts about 1 gram of carbs per slice, it is best to avoid all breads. For now, eliminate grains, breads, pasta, starches, potatoes, corn, rice, oats, and cereals. A single cup of pasta, for example, has 44 grams of carbs, more than enough to knock you out of the Keto Zone for the entire day. And a single slice of whole-wheat bread typically has 20 grams of carbs, your limit for the day.

How can I lower my stress levels?

People who are stressed have increased cortisol, which can trigger adrenalin, which can cause elevated blood sugar levels. That may also bump you out of the Keto Zone. If you are stressed, do things that are fun, laugh, get counseling, take a break, or get exercise. For more information on how to cope with stress, refer to my book *Stress Less*.

Do I have to eat three meals a day?

Some people will only want two meals a day. Some may even go down to a single meal a day, along with their Keto Zone coffee (which includes MCT oil powder or oil, avocado oil, and grass-fed butter), but it is up to you. As long as you are getting your necessary fats and proteins and green veggie carbs and are staying in the Keto Zone, you can decide for yourself how often to eat. Typically the more snacks you eat, the less weight you lose. MCT oil can cause diarrhea, while MCT oil powder rarely does.

> **IT'S A FACT**
>
> The best day of the week to start the Keto Zone diet: Saturday morning.

How much exercise is required?

Exercise helps you stay in the Keto Zone. It also speeds up your weight loss, boosts energy, burns fat, increases muscle, and revs up your metabolic rate, which means increased fat burning when you are resting. Technically, it takes a 3,500-calorie deficit to lose a pound of fat, so if you burn an extra 500 calories per day with exercise, in a week that is an extra pound of fat loss. A brisk walk twenty to thirty minutes a day, five times a week, is usually sufficient to accomplish this. By being in the Keto Zone, you will lose about one to two pounds a week anyway. Adding exercise usually increases that to two to three pounds of fat loss per week.

Is there a special way to cook all this healthy food?

Cooking over low heat is important. The higher the heat, the more denatured, oxidized, and damaged the food becomes, and that means fewer health benefits. Never cook with polyunsaturated fats (soybean oil, corn oil, grape-seed oil, etc.). The best cooking oil is ghee, grass-fed butter, avocado oil, or coconut oil. When you broil or grill, use lower heat, and do not burn or char the meat. Veggies are best steamed or sautéed. Bake at 320 degrees or less, use a slow cooker, and do not use a microwave to cook food. Eggs are good poached, soft boiled, or over easy. If you scramble your eggs, use low heat so you do not oxidize the yolk.

How soon will I see results with my cholesterol numbers?

I recommend that you get a lipid panel test done three to four months after you start your Keto Zone diet. If your LDL numbers are not significantly improved, you should request an NMR Lipoprofile to see which LDL numbers (pattern A or pattern B) are elevated. But usually, within three to four months, there is a marked improvement: LDL numbers are usually mildly increased, triglycerides are usually way down, and HDL is usually up. The bad pattern B LDL cholesterol is usually decreased, but the neutral pattern A LDL cholesterol is usually increased. (Refer to chapter 6 and appendix D for more information.)

How much is all this going to cost me?
Fats are cheap, and with 70 percent of the diet being fats, it likely will be less expensive than you think. The protein, 10 to 15 percent of the diet, is the most expensive part, but we are not eating all that much protein. The remaining 15 percent is green veggies, also pretty cheap. All in all, the Keto Zone diet is very economical. It may even save you money.

OFF TO THE RACES

You are ready to jump into the Keto Zone diet. You know what it looks like, you know what to expect, and I hope your questions have been answered.

The exact foods, how much of each, even menu options, all of that is coming.

The key thing is that you are ready.

Remember, falling out of the Keto Zone diet can only happen for a limited number of reasons: not enough fats, too much protein, or too many carbs.

That is it. So as long as you stick to the Keto Zone path, you will be right where you want to be—in the fat-burning mode—and you won't have to worry about counting calories.

So relax and enjoy the ride.

———————————————

"Starting out with the right foods
really helps me stay focused
on the diet."
—Joanne

———————————————

CHAPTER THIRTEEN

GO SHOPPING FOR THE RIGHT INGREDIENTS

IT WAS NOT QUITE SLEEPWALKING, but it was certainly in a daze that Kathy walked toward the refrigerator late at night. "I absolutely had to have something to eat," she told me later. "I could not sleep. All I could think about was food . . . food . . . food, especially that ice cream."

Clearly, something was wrong. Kathy knew it, and her weight proved it, but she did not know what to do. All her previous attempts at dieting had ended in what she called a "catastrophe."

"Did you clear out your freezer or fridge or pantry before you started a diet?" I asked.

She looked at me a little confused. "No, I never did that before," she replied. "I don't think I would want to throw out all that good food. Besides, my husband would not be too happy about that."

I explained, "Some foods are pretty addicting. Did you know that sugar has been found in some studies to be more addictive than cocaine? So if you leave sugary foods in the house, it will be incredibly hard to resist it. You are putting yourself in a very difficult situation. As for your husband, for a season, he might be okay with it. Try it. See what he says."

Kathy went home and that night, with the help of her husband, went through their entire kitchen and pantry. Some things they threw out; others they gave away. Her husband even stashed a few boxes of Girl Scout cookies in the garage in his top cabinet, but because she thought they were thrown away, that worked for her.

Then she went out and restocked her shelves with Keto Zone–friendly foods.

A few weeks later she called my office. "I still plan to come in next week, but I wanted to tell you in advance that it is working," she beamed. "Not only is my body satisfied and not starving on the Keto Zone diet, but my mind is so calm. I think it's because I know there is no escape, no secret stash of comfort foods anywhere in the house. And I have already lost eight pounds!"

I could almost see her smiling through the phone.

> **IT'S A FACT**
>
> Evenings are usually the time when foods are the most tempting.

CLEANING HOUSE

There is great wisdom in clearing out your freezer, fridge, and pantry of foods that will bump you out of the Keto Zone or that are simply not healthy.

As the saying goes, "Out of sight, out of mind." It really is true, especially when it comes to eating. This is your body, your health, and your weight loss, and I strongly suggest that you clear things out and start fresh, but it is also your house, so you are the one to make that call.

For many people, having the same old comfort foods around

the house will be a temptation that is extremely hard to resist. Just get rid of them, or take them to the home of a relative, friend, or neighbor. You do not need the extra temptation.

On clean-out day, here are some of the things that need to go:

- *Boxed food:* Get rid of packaged, processed foods in a bag or box. They contain too many carbs, sugars, artificial sweeteners, hydrogenated oils, or refined oils to keep you in the Keto Zone. That means no pasta, breads, bagels, pretzels, chips, cereals, cookies, or frozen desserts.
- *Wheat, grains, beans:* Get rid of all flour, grains, rye, oats, corn, wheat, popcorn, barley, rice, brown rice, beans, peas, hummus, and lentils whether dried or in cans.
- *Unhealthy oils and fats:* Margarine, soy, and oils (sunflower, cottonseed, canola, soybean, corn, grape-seed, rapeseed, or safflower) need to go.
- *Canned goods:* Foods in metal cans, especially canned veggies, are notorious for containing BPA (bisphenol A), which disrupts our hormones.[82] By imitating estrogen, it can fool the body into thinking that it is estrogen. In research, animals exposed to low levels of BPA had higher rates of diabetes, breast and prostate cancer, reproductive problems, low sperm count, obesity, and other negative effects. Not all canned food contains BPA, but they do contain unhealthy additives (to extend shelf life) and sugary juices (with many fruits and veggies) that can bump you out of the Keto Zone.
- *Sugar and artificial sweeteners:* Get rid of them all. Artificial sweeteners are unhealthy and mess with your appetite hormones. Regular sugar should be removed, or put away if it is not too tempting. For now, use stevia or monk fruit (lo

han guo powder or liquid) or sweet alcohols (erythritol and xylitol) because these are healthy and low carb.

- *Dairy:* Other than hard cheeses, heavy whipping cream, cream cheese, and grass-fed butter, all other dairy should go. It is best to choose organic dairy and to alternate consuming dairy every three to four days.
- *Low-fat:* Foods labeled "low-fat" or "fat-free" are usually especially bad for you because of added sugar and almost always throw you out of the Keto Zone.
- *Sauces and condiments:* Most sauces and condiments, like ketchup, have sugars, so avoid them entirely or read the label and use sparingly. Spices such as pepper, salt, onion, garlic, and herbs are fine and have very low to virtually no carbs.
- *Beverages:* Get rid of all sodas, sport drinks, smoothies, sweetened coffees and teas, and drinks with artificial sweeteners.
- *Fruit juices:* Fresh-squeezed orange juice, though delicious, is very high in sugar. It instantly will sabotage your diet and bump you out of the Keto Zone. Remove *all* fruit juices.
- *Alcohol:* It is just best to cut out all alcohol. It will mess with your daily carb intake limit and bump you out of the Keto Zone. It also gives you brain fog and food cravings, and it reduces your ability to resist cravings. For now, just remove it from the diet.
- *Fruit:* Fruits like bananas, grapes, mangos, oranges, peaches, pears, pineapples, and plums, though delicious and healthy, contain too much sugar for you to stay in the Keto Zone.
- *Dried fruits:* Dried fruits, though natural and healthy, are high in fructose. For now, cut them out.
- *Jams, jellies, and preserves:* These have way too much sugar.

- *Chocolate and candy:* Except for 85 percent or higher low-sugar dark chocolate or dark chocolate with stevia, no other chocolate or candy works with the Keto Zone diet.
- *Some vegetables need to go as well:* Carrots, potatoes, beets, sweet potatoes, yams, and winter squashes (like acorn and butternut) have to go, as they are starches.

When you have pulled all these foods out and piled them on the kitchen table, make sure you throw out the foods you know you are addicted to and that may sabotage your diet. This includes the foods you know are unhealthy. It is not worth the risk to keep them in the house.

However, if there are foods you can avoid, such as a jar of home-made blueberry jam, a bottle of unopened wine, a tub of baking flour, or some other food item, then keep them. This is not about being cruel and heartless or throwing out things you value and may someday want again. Keep them. Store them away. That is fine. Only you know yourself, so if something is too tempting, then get rid of it. Your diet and your health are more important than anything you might have placed on the kitchen table.

> **IT'S A FACT**
>
> "Pasteurized milk competes only with gluten as the most allergic substance in the Western diet."
> –Dave Asprey, author of *The Bulletproof Diet*

If you have healthy foods (like spinach) that are frozen rather than raw, that is fine. Keep them. Food in glass jars is fine as well. I would, however, steer clear of metal cans, especially with tomato products.

Now that you have the shelves empty, it is time to restock them.

RESTOCKING YOUR SHELVES

You are looking to get in the Keto Zone as quickly as possible, for it is the optimum fat-burning zone as well as the peak performance and health zone, and to stay there for as long as you desire. That is the primary goal of the foods you will buy to restock your shelves.

I find keeping that goal right in front of my mind is especially important when getting rid of certain foods, especially comfort foods, and grabbing hold of new foods. Letting go of foods is admittedly not comfortable, but it is and will be great for your body.

The intake of 70 percent fats, 15 percent proteins, and 15 percent green veggie carbs is the framework, but the actual ingredients you choose are up to you. Here is a good outline to begin with:

IT'S A FACT

Net carbs: subtract fiber from total carb count. For example, ¼ cup of sliced strawberries has about 3 total carbs and 1 fiber carb, so 3 - 1 = 2 net carbs.

PROTEINS (15 PERCENT)

You know the ratio of protein you need per day (1 gram of protein per 2.2 pounds you weigh) and therefore how much protein you need per meal.

- 250 pounds: 114 g. protein per day = 38 g. per meal (5 to 6 oz. protein)
- 180 pounds: 80 g. protein per day = 27 g. per meal (4 oz. protein)

- 150 pounds: 68 g. protein   (3 to 3.5 oz. protein)
  per day = 23 g. per meal

Remember that 1 ounce of protein from egg, fish, chicken, or steak is approximately 7 grams of protein. That makes the math pretty easy. Per meal, that is about 3 to 4 ounces of protein for women and 3 to 6 ounces of protein for men. How you choose to meet that need is up to you.

Fish (wild is best and low in mercury)

- Wild salmon
- Halibut
- Anchovies
- Perch
- Pollock
- Sole
- Tilapia
- Trout
- Herring
- Sardines
- Tuna (tongol)
- Flounder

Shellfish (wild is better than farm-raised)

- Clams
- Scallops
- Oysters
- Shrimp
- Squid
- Crab

Poultry

- Eggs (pastured organic is best)
- Chicken
- Duck
- Goose
- Cornish hen
- Quail
- Pheasant
- Turkey

Meat (grass-fed organic is best)

- Beef
- Goat
- Lamb
- Pork
- Veal
- Venison

Dairy (grass-fed organic is best).

Remember, even though dairy and nuts are listed under protein, they include carbs that count toward your 20 grams per day limit. The carb numbers here are net carbs (total carbs – fiber = net carbs).

- Grass-fed butter: 2 Tbsp., 1 g. net carb
- Organic cheese: 4 oz. per day maximum, 1 g. net carb per ounce
- Organic cream cheese: 2 Tbsp., 0.8 g. net carb
- Full cream (heavy whipping cream), 0 g. net carb

Nuts

- Almond milk: 1 cup, 1 g. net carb
- Coconut milk: 1 cup, 1 g. net carb
- Almonds: 24 nuts, 2.3 g. net carbs
- Almond butter: 1 Tbsp., 2.5 g. net carbs
- Cashews: 9 nuts, 4.3 g. net carbs
- Peanuts: 22 nuts, 1.5 g. net carbs
- Peanut butter: 1 Tbsp., 2.4 g. net carbs (avoid most processed peanut butter since they usually contain hydrogenated fats)
- Pecans: 10 whole (1 oz.), 4 g. net carbs
- Macadamia: 8 medium-size nuts (1 oz.), 4 g. net carbs
- Hazelnuts: 20 nuts, 4.5 g. net carbs

- Walnuts: 10 whole (1 oz.), 3 g. net carbs
- Coconut: fresh shredded (½ cup), 6 g. net carbs
- Coconut: unsweetened dried (1 oz.), 7 g. net carbs
- Coconut cream butter: 2 Tbsp., 2 g. net carbs

Raw whole nuts are best, but roasted is fine. If nuts cause flu-like symptoms, then stop eating them or use them sparingly. Note that some nuts, such as cashews, are higher in carbs. Excessive intake of nuts or consuming higher-carb nuts such as cashews (and peanuts, even though it is a legume) can throw you out of the Keto Zone and may rarely trigger flu-like symptoms for some.

IT'S A FACT

Coconut cream butter is made by blending coconut in a high-speed blender, creating a consistency similar to peanut butter (2 tablespoons of coconut butter contain 17 grams of fat and 2 grams of net carbs). Coconut cream or coconut butter is usually thicker, richer, and sweeter than coconut milk and may be used as a dairy substitute for desserts, smoothies, and soups. The cream that rises to the top of a can of coconut milk is the coconut cream.

VEGETABLES (15 PERCENT)

Basically, think salad vegetables and vegetables that you would cook. Salads are measured in cups (1 cup), while cooked vegetables are measured in half cups (½ cup).

Roughly speaking, you are going to eat about 2 to 6 cups of salad and 1 to 2 cups of cooked veggies per day, but you can usually eat as much as you want of green leafy veggies, and use generous amounts of extra-virgin olive oil (2 to 3 tablespoons) and apple cider vinegar in a ratio of three parts olive oil to one part apple cider vinegar. Here are many of the common vegetables you can enjoy. The carb numbers listed here are net carbs.

Raw Veggies (organic is best)
- Avocado: 3 slices, 1 oz., 2 g. net carbs
- Avocado: 2 Tbsp. mashed, 1 oz., 2 g. net carbs
- Broccoli pieces: 1 cup, 1.6 g. net carbs
- Green beans: 1 cup, 4.2 g. net carbs
- Cabbage: 1 cup, 2.2 g. net carbs
- Celery: 1 rib, 0.8 g. net carb
- Cucumber: 1 cup, 2 g. net carbs
- Mixed greens: 1 cup, 0.4 g. net carb
- Black olives: 5 count, 0.7 g. net carb
- Green olives: 5 count, 0 g. net carb
- Onion: 2 Tbsp. chopped, 1.5 g. net carbs
- Green pepper: 1 cup, 4.2 g. net carbs
- Romaine lettuce: 1 cup, 0.4 g. net carb
- Spinach: 1 cup, 0.2 g. net carb
- Tomato: 1 small (3 to 4 oz.), 2.5 g. net carbs

Cooked Veggies
- Green beans: ½ cup, 2.9 g. net carbs
- Bok choy: ½ cup, 0.2 g. net carb
- Broccoli: ½ cup, 1.7 g. net carbs
- Brussels sprouts: ½ cup, 3.6 g. net carbs
- Cauliflower: ½ cup, 0.9 g. net carb
- Collard greens: ½ cup, 2 g. net carbs

- Eggplant: ½ cup, 2 g. net carbs
- Kale: ½ cup, 2.4 g. net carbs
- Button mushrooms: ½ cup, 4.6 g. net carbs (caution with amount)
- Onion: ½ cup, 8.6 g. net carbs (caution with amount)
- Green pepper: ½ cup, 3.8 g. net carbs
- Snow peas: ½ cup, 3.4 g. net carbs
- Spinach: ½ cup, 2.2 g. net carbs
- Tomato: ½ cup, 8.6 g. net carbs (caution with amount)
- Zucchini: ½ cup, 1.5 g. net carbs

OILS (70 PERCENT)

Oils have no carbs so they are ideal for food satisfaction, decreasing hunger and cravings, sticking to the 20 gram carb limit, and providing your body with the optimal fuel source.

Extra-virgin olive oil and avocado oil are ideal for salad dressings. You can cook with coconut oil, avocado oil, ghee, and grass-fed butter. These oils are also good for sautéing.

MCT oil is not only great for increasing energy, but it also pushes you into the Keto Zone. The fat from MCT oil is not stored; it only burns as fuel. I recommend it especially in your coffee

> ### IT'S A FACT
>
> It's old news, but fake fats make us fat.[83]

in the mornings (1 to 2 tablespoons). I prefer the MCT oil powder for my coffee. Start with the lower amount of MCT to avoid loose stools.

These are ideal healthy oils (serving size with oils is 1 tablespoon) for the Keto Zone. You can also choose nut butters.

Saturated Fats (best for cooking)
- Grass-fed butter
- Extra-virgin coconut oil
- MCT oil (powder, liquid, or capsule)
- Ghee (clarified butter, grass-fed)
- Palm oil (sustainable only)
- Cocoa butter (usually not for cooking)

Monounsaturated Fats
- Extra-virgin olive oil
- Avocado oil
- Almond oil
- Macadamia nut oil

MISCELLANEOUS

From spices to fruits to beverages, these foods, separate from fats, veggies, and proteins, are safe to eat on the Keto Zone diet. Be sure to include their carb count in your daily 20 gram limit.

Fruits
- Blueberries fresh: ¼ cup, 4.1 g. net carbs
- Blueberries frozen: ¼ cup, 3.7 g. net carbs
- Blackberries fresh: ¼ cup, 2.7 g. net carbs
- Blackberries frozen: ¼ cup, 4.1 g. net carbs
- Raspberries fresh: ¼ cup, 1.5 g. net carbs
- Raspberries frozen: ¼ cup, 1.8 g. net carbs
- Strawberries fresh, sliced: ¼ cup, 1.8 g. net carbs
- Strawberries frozen: ¼ cup, 2.6 g. net carbs
- Lemon juice: 2 Tbsp., 2.1 g. net carbs
- Lime juice: 2 Tbsp., 2.6 g. net carbs

Beverages
- Water
- Sparkling water
- Coffee
- Green tea
- Black tea
- Yerba mate
- Nut milks (almond and coconut have low sugar)

Nut milks are low carb and good to use in smoothies. Just be sure to use the low-carb types with 1 gram or less of carbs per 8-ounce serving.

Supplements
- A comprehensive multivitamin with vitamin D (1000 to 2000 IU) and magnesium (400 mg) a day
- Omega-3 (EPA/DHA) 1 to 2 g. per day and/or krill oil (350 to 1000 mg) per day
- Electrolyte packets: in first month of Keto Zone, people often need extra magnesium, sodium, and potassium
- A digestive enzyme with extra lipase to help with the digestion of fats, especially for those fifty-five and older

Spices and Condiments
- Garlic: 1 large clove, 0.9 g. net carbs
- Ginger: 1 Tbsp., 0.8 g. net carbs
- Pesto sauce: 1 Tbsp., 0.6 g. net carbs
- Apple cider vinegar: 1 Tbsp., 1 g. net carbs
- Sea salt: 1 tsp., 0 g. net carb
- Himalayan salt (pink): 1 tsp., 0 g. net carb
- Rosemary: 1 tsp., 1 g. net carb

- Turmeric: 1 tsp., 1 g. net carb
- Oregano: 1 tsp., 1 g. net carb
- Thyme: 1 tsp., 1 g. net carb
- Black pepper: 1 tsp., 0.5 g. net carb
- Vanilla extract: 1 tsp., 0.5 g. net carb
- Cinnamon 1 tsp., 2 g. net carbs

EATING OUT AND STAYING IN THE KETO ZONE

You can eat out and stay in the Keto Zone. You may have to bring your own olive oil or avocado oil and apple cider vinegar or grass-fed butter (as I do), but it is certainly doable.

Whether you are traveling or just going out to eat, you can make it work and keep yourself in the Keto Zone.

Eating out is also a good way to treat yourself. For a long while, every Monday night Mary and I would go out to eat at a local restaurant and have a salad with mozzarella cheese, tomatoes, basil, olive oil, a little balsamic vinegar, and a lot of herbs and spices. It is called a Caprese salad. It was delicious, and we both stayed in the Keto Zone.

Whether it is breakfast, lunch, or dinner, get creative and make the restaurant's menu fit your Keto Zone diet.

If you happen to get bumped out of the Keto Zone, you may feel it the next day. That is fine. Just get back into it, and usually within a day you will be back in the groove.

IT'S A FACT

When you eat grain-fed steak, choose the leaner cuts, such as a fillet, but when choosing grass-fed steak, it is usually best to choose the fattier cuts, such as a rib eye.

AN EASY PLACE TO START

To get started, you will need several basics. I call it a "Keto Zone starter kit," but it is just a combination of basic ingredients that will help restock your fridge and pantry with foods that will get you in the Keto Zone and keep you there.

With every person who is about to dive into the Keto Zone diet, I suggest this easy outline:

Fats, Oils, and Nuts
- MCT oil powder (500 ml)
- Extra-virgin olive oil (1 to 2 qt.)
- Grass-fed butter (3 to 4 sticks, or 3/4 to 1 lb.) or ghee
- Extra-virgin coconut oil
- Avocado oil
- Avocados
- Almonds, pecans, macadamia nuts, walnuts, or peanuts (2 to 3 cans of each)
- Cream cheese
- Organic cheese
- Sea salt and vinegar peanuts (a life-saver for my wife) (2 to 3 cans)
- Olive oil or avocado oil mayonnaise
- Organic peanut butter and almond butter
- Heavy cream (1 to 2 pints)

Proteins
- Pastured organic eggs (2 dozen)
- Grass-fed beef (12 oz. or more)
- Grass-fed rib eye

- Prepared tuna and chicken salad (keep in fridge)
- Pastured chicken (12 oz. or more)
- Tongol tuna
- Pastured turkey
- Wild shrimp
- Wild salmon fillets
- Smoked salmon

Green Vegetables
- Salad veggies such as romaine, spinach, field greens, arugula, mixed greens (a couple tubs or bags)
- Other raw veggies: cucumbers, peppers, tomatoes, onions, olives (as much as you like and want), broccoli, cauliflower, cabbage, Brussels sprouts
- Veggies to cook (as much as you like and want). Frozen are fine.

Beverages
- Coffee (single source if you can)
- Tea (black, green)
- Water (spring, filtered, sparkling, or alkaline)
- Almond milk, low sugar (1/2 gal.)
- Coconut milk, low sugar (1/2 gal.)

Miscellaneous
- Apple cider vinegar (2 bottles)
- Dark chocolate, low-sugar or sweetened with stevia, 85% cacao or higher (3 bars)
- Salt: Himalayan salt or sea salt (1 box)

- Supplements such as a good multivitamin, vitamin D3, magnesium (see appendix A)
- Omega-3 oil and/or krill oil, 1 capsule twice a day of either (see appendix A)
- A digestive enzyme with extra lipase (see appendix A)

As you go, week by week, you will get a feel for the foods and your preferences. Eventually you will be able to rotate foods every three to four days so that you are enjoying your meals while also getting the necessary fats, proteins, and green veggies.

The goal, of course, is to stay in the Keto Zone.

The 20 gram carb limit is going to be the line in the sand that you do not cross. In time, you will be able to push the 20 grams of carbs to 50 grams and then more, but for now, keep it low so that you maximize the Keto Zone and its fat-burning power.

"My morning coffee
with MCT oil powder and avocado oil . . .
makes me feel great
and satisfied for four hours."
—*Brian*

CHAPTER FOURTEEN
GET IN THE KETO ZONE

CLOCKING IN AT ALMOST three hundred pounds, Dave really needed to lose weight. His doctors agreed with him, and sooner rather than later! He had medical conditions that made a heart attack or stroke look probable.

Willing to try most anything, Dave went to work on himself unconventionally. He restricted his calorie intake for more than a year, but the weight did not come off. He tried exercising more than an hour a day, six days a week, and though he became stronger, the fat remained.

Frustrated, he dug even deeper. It turns out his body, among other things, was very carbohydrate sensitive. When he learned about a ketogenic diet, he kept lowering and lowering his carb intake until he finally reached ketosis. For the first time in his life, the fat melted away.

Today, Dave Asprey is a new man, having lost those stubborn one hundred pounds. He went on to create a very powerful tool for those on ketogenic diets, like the Keto Zone diet. His creation, which he called "Bulletproof Coffee" (outlined in his book, *The*

Bulletproof Diet) is a very healthy way to start the day. I recommend it. His coffee recipe includes:

- Single-source coffee (coffee from one location, not a mix of coffees from several locations), which is most likely low in mold toxins
- 1 Tbsp. unsalted, grass-fed butter (or ghee)
- 1 Tbsp. MCT oil
- Optional cinnamon, vanilla powder, chocolate powder, or stevia

Blend these ingredients together. (Stir the ingredients together if you are on the go, but blending is the best option.) The oil and butter suppress hunger, and the coffee gives your brain the boost it needs. The mixture becomes a rich, smooth drink that helps your metabolism continue to burn fats for hours.

Your ketone levels at night are pushed forward into the day, plus you feel energized as you start the day.

IN THE KETO ZONE

When you are in the Keto Zone, you are burning fat generally without hunger or food cravings. You are losing belly fat, and your appetite hormones are usually balanced. You typically have incredible amounts of energy, along with mental clarity and focus. You are cruising!

I have had some patients say, "I feel like I'm eighteen years old again." The young and optimistic feelings return. In many ways, the Keto Zone diet usually becomes like an antidepressant and feel-good diet all in one.

On top of that, results are normally fast. The average person loses four to five pounds of fluid weight the first week, followed usually by one to two pounds of fat per week after that. Throw in some exercise and replace breakfast with a Bulletproof Coffee or ketogenic coffee, and many will lose one pound of fat per day. I personally prefer my ketogenic coffee using avocado oil and MCT oil powder over Bulletproof Coffee because it will not raise your LDL cholesterol level but will usually raise the good HDL cholesterol. I also add ¼ teaspoon of sugar-free dark cocoa powder.

All of this without increased appetite, insatiable food cravings, weight gain, or counting calories!

That is pretty incredible right there, considering what people usually experience when they are losing weight.

I know one man whose KCL number was somewhere down near 10 grams of carbs per day. That is extremely low. The point is, if he were eating 20 grams a day on the Keto Zone diet, he would no doubt complain that "it's not working."

Sometimes questions do arise.

You have to consider the fact that your body is transitioning from a sugar-burning engine to a fat-burning engine. All the carb spikes and insulin bursts have ceased. Insulin, the key hormone that tells your body to store fat, is now virtually silenced. The fat-storage cycle has been broken. That is quite a change. Thankfully, your body can handle it, but some hiccups are to be expected. With most of my patients on the Keto Zone diet, I have found that when their fasting serum insulin level reaches 3.0 mcU/mL (microunits per milliliter) or preferably lower, weight loss is fast and easy. Yet most doctors don't check serum insulin levels.

> **IT'S A FACT**
>
> Your body thinks fat storage is more important than fat burning. Being in the Keto Zone changes that.

Also, withdrawals are a very real factor for many people. Sugars and carbohydrates are usually addictive, and now all the rules and routines are changing!

Most likely, it will only take your body one to five days to reach the Keto Zone. At that point you will begin to see ketones in your urine test strips, and you will feel the change taking place. For some, it may take longer to reach the Keto Zone, perhaps a week or two. If you have type 2 diabetes, it may take two to four weeks to hit the Keto Zone.

If you feel like your body is rebelling, remember this: *you will get there!* Below are some practical tips that may help you break into the Keto Zone—and stay there—if your body gives you some resistance.

BREAKING THROUGH

How your body will react to this overall shift from fat storage to fat burning is really unknown. Your body is unique, as is your KCL number (you will know your KCL number soon), but usually the process is fast, almost like flipping a switch.

> ### IT'S A FACT
> You want your ketone levels at 0.5 to 5 millimolars. That is the fat-burning Keto Zone.

The biggest obstacle, if it even occurs at all for you, is called the "gray zone" by some, the "keto flu" by others, or "the week I locked my keys in the car" by another. It is bothersome, but not dangerous.

Have you ever tried to run through water or snow that is knee-deep? You can do it, but it is slow going. If your body is not burning sugars well and not yet burning fats well, it will feel like you are stuck in this yucky slow-motion mess—fatigue, bad breath, frequent urination, headaches, brain fog, weird symptoms (locking keys in car), constipation, gas, aching muscles, and even a tough time sleeping.

The answer is simple: *get out as quickly as you can!*

Rest assured, this is not what the Keto Zone feels like, nor is it what the transition process entails. This is being stuck between burning sugar as your fuel and burning fat as your fuel. You need to press through as fast as possible so you can enjoy the benefits of the Keto Zone.

If you are stuck: Examine your food intake. Are you eating too many carbs? Not getting enough fats? Eating too much protein? Make sure you are at or below your 20 grams daily carb limit. Some type 2 diabetics may need to lower their carb intake to 10 grams a day.

If you are in need or want a good push: Take an additional 1 tablespoon of MCT oil powder or oil at meals. The MCT (medium-chain triglyceride) oil pushes you into the Keto Zone quickly. You can choose MCT oil powder, capsule, or liquid.

Usually, by increasing fats, including MCT oil, and lowering carbs and sometimes proteins, the body surges ahead past the flu-like symptoms. You will then find yourself right where you want to be—enjoying all the benefits of the Keto Zone.

There really is no way to keep your body from reaching the Keto Zone as long as your carb intake is low enough for you, protein intake is low to moderate, and the necessary fat intake is high. You will get there eventually, but faster is better in this case.

TROUBLESHOOTING IF NEEDED

Because everyone is different, people have varying questions and concerns as they transition into the Keto Zone. Here are some of the most common:

What if I get light-headed, have brain fog, or feel sluggish?
You probably need sodium in the form of salted almonds or other salted nuts, a clear broth soup (like bouillon), or an electrolyte packet containing sodium, magnesium, and potassium. You may also need to increase your sea salt or Himalayan salt intake.

What if I get constipated?
You need more water (1 to 2 quarts per day at least), fiber (from veggies), and magnesium (200 milligrams twice a day is normal, double if constipated). Increasing olive oil intake will also help.

What if I get diarrhea, bloating, or gas?
This will usually stop after a couple days as your body adjusts to the new high-fat diet. You can decrease magnesium a bit since it may trigger diarrhea in some people. Taking too much MCT oil or olive oil can also trigger diarrhea. Cut back your dose of these oils if diarrhea occurs, and when it stops, increase the dose slowly and gradually.

People over age fifty-five may need a digestive enzyme containing extra lipase to help them digest fats better and to curb diarrhea.

What if I have eye twitches, heart flutters, or muscle cramps?
You probably need more magnesium or potassium. A handful of nuts is high in magnesium. Or you can take 400 milligrams of chelated magnesium supplement. Half an avocado contains twice the

potassium of a banana, and without the carbs. (A banana will bump you out of the Keto Zone.) Again, an electrolyte packet will help if it contains magnesium, potassium, and sodium.

What if I get hungry while on the diet?

If you are hungry, it is because you are not eating enough fats (or too many carbs or too much protein). You can eat 1 to 2 tablespoons of almond butter, a couple slices of full-fat cheese, a lettuce-wrapped burger wrapped (no bun) with 1 to 2 slices of cheese, or even a chicken breast with 1 to 2 slices of cheese. That will knock out the hunger and keep your carb intake low.

What if I eat or drink something and then feel groggy?

That food or drink (for example, peanuts, coffee, cheese, whipping cream, etc.) may be causing you inflammation. You could be sensitive to it, or it may contain mold toxins or other toxins, or perhaps what you ate was simply too high in carbs. Minimize it if you can, avoid it if you need to, and keep your carb intake at 20 grams or lower per day.

What if I urinate a lot more than normal?

When your body shifts into ketosis, insulin levels go down. The elevated insulin has caused you to retain water, so you will lose about four to five pounds of water weight your first week in the Keto Zone as your kidneys excrete the excess fluids. Drink sufficient water (usually 2 quarts a day for the first week and 1 to 2 quarts thereafter), along with taking sodium, potassium, and magnesium, during this time. The frequent urination will usually stop after the first week. Also, for the first week, you may need to urinate one to two times during the night.

What if I am not getting enough fiber?
Fiber is important, but you will usually get plenty with the veggies on the Keto Zone diet. You can add seeds (for example, chia seeds or psyllium seeds, 1 tablespoon one to two times per day) in a few weeks, but seeds also have carbs. For now, the fiber in the green vegetables will usually be sufficient.

What if I feel achy?
Again, the foods you are eating may be causing inflammation. Peanuts, foods high in mold toxins (such as moldy nuts and moldy berries), and dairy are common causes. Alternate dairy every three to four days or avoid altogether. There are other food and drink choices.

What if I eat too many carbs by accident?
You are usually only twelve hours to one day away from getting back on track. Relax. You can usually be back in the Keto Zone the next day—especially if you use MCT oil powder or MCT oil, which puts you right into ketosis.

What if my gallbladder acts up?
Often women who have done a lot of low-fat diets and vegetarians may have gallbladder issues without realizing it. Their gallbladder may contain sludge or may not be functioning properly since fats usually help the gallbladder function better. Healthy fats, such as 1 to 2 tablespoons of olive oil two to three times a day, will usually flush out the gallbladder.

Initially, you may need a teaspoon of olive oil every hour, for four to eight hours, to slowly get the gallbladder functioning normally again. Take it slow if you need to, and consult your doctor if the pain persists; you may have undiagnosed gallstones or sludge in your gallbladder.

What if my four pounds of water loss comes back?
When you first went into the Keto Zone, your body probably dumped about four pounds of stored water and glycogen. If you bump yourself out of the Keto Zone, it is possible that you may suddenly gain that water back from a single meal (by eating pizza or a baked potato, for example). Though it may seem scary, you know what happened. Stick to the Keto Zone diet, and you will lose those 4 pounds of water in no time.

What if I get depressed?
On a low-carb diet such as the Keto Zone, some people develop low serotonin levels, and that may bring on mild depression, feeling down, or food cravings. This typically occurs more often with women than men. An amino acid 5HTP (50 to 150 milligrams) or L-tryptophan (500 to 1000 milligrams) at bedtime will usually do wonders. Both are available at health food stores.

> ### IT'S A FACT
>
> Common symptoms of low serotonin include insomnia, craving starches and sweets, depressed moods, low self-esteem, and anxiety.

What if I am taking other mediations?
One major benefit of the Keto Zone diet is the fact that your body will usually begin to heal in many ways. If you are taking medication for hypertension, diabetes, arthritis, or high cholesterol, you will need to follow up with your physician regularly to see if your dosage needs to be lowered or even discontinued.

What if I cannot sleep?

Make sure your last coffee or tea in the day is not after 2 or 3 p.m. That can interfere with sleep. 5HTP or L-tryptophan at night can help. One benefit of the Keto Zone diet is increased energy and, for many, the decreased need for sleep. When you sleep, it should be sound, but you may need less sleep as time progresses. Also try taking your magnesium supplement at bedtime since magnesium helps many with insomnia.

What is the worst that could happen to me?

Apart from the Keto Zone diet helping you uncover a medical issue (like gallstones) you already have, the diet usually should not cause you any harm. It is incredibly healthy, not to mention being the ideal way to lose weight. I do not recommend the Keto Zone diet for expectant mothers since it will prevent necessary weight gain during pregnancy.

GET YOURSELF INTO THE KETO ZONE!

The goal is, of course, to get you into the Keto Zone as quickly as possible so you can enjoy and maximize the many benefits. Most likely, you will transition quickly from sugar-burning to fat-burning. Do all you can to get yourself into the Keto Zone.

> ### IT'S A FACT
>
> Is corn oil healthy? It does lower cholesterol, but it oxidizes cholesterol and may eventually cause plaque in the arteries.

If you develop any of these symptoms, go back to the most likely cause: food intake. Then increase your fats and decrease your carbs and protein.

And give yourself a jump-start with MCT oil powder or MCT oil.

It will usually help you speed into the Keto Zone and bypass the potential stuck-between sugar-burning and fat-burning "keto flu" symptoms.

If you are worried the transition process may affect your work performance, then simply start on a Friday afternoon. You will probably be well into the Keto Zone come Monday morning.

The Keto Zone diet mix—70 percent fats, 15 percent protein, 15 percent green veggie carbs—is vitally important. Using this as your primary fuel source is perfect for burning fat, all without hunger, cravings, and runaway appetite hormones.

Burning fat all day and all night, while feeling good, sleeping great, reversing countless diseases, and quenching inflammation and oxidation—what else could you ask for?

One thing would make this even easier: a full list of foods, menus, and recipes.

That is the next chapter.

"I used your recipes and advice
to lose 50 pounds!"
—*Dan*

CHAPTER FIFTEEN

STAY IN THE KETO ZONE WITH THE RIGHT MENU PLANS

BARBARA WAS A PATIENT who had gained about fifty pounds over a period of five years. Before she came to see me, she had been on a commercial diet plan for about six months and had not lost any weight. She continually had a ravenous appetite.

During her appointment, I discovered that she drank a diet soda for lunch and dinner. She also usually drank another diet soda in the afternoon as a pick-me-up. She also chewed sugar-free gum throughout the day, which also contained artificial sweeteners.

"I'm doing the right thing, aren't I?" she asked. "Neither the diet soda nor the sugar-free gum has any calories, so it must be helping me, right?"

I explained, "Actually, diet sodas usually trigger appetite and cause carb and sugar cravings."

She started on the Keto Zone diet, removing diet soda and sugar-free gum from her diet, and she lost fifty pounds in about six months without any effort at all. She was amazed.

What is more, her once-ravenous appetite was completely under control.

Barbara had no idea what her diet drinks and sugar-free gum were doing to her body. By removing them and getting into the Keto Zone, her body quickly turned around. It was amazing to watch, and she loved every minute of it.

Staying in the Keto Zone is easy, especially when you have plenty of meal options to choose from. All you need to do is follow these meal options and rotate them as desired. You will be in the Keto Zone, enjoying all of its benefits.

Just follow these meal plans, rotating them every few days, and you will usually stay right in the middle of the Keto Zone!

BREAKFASTS

#1—Eggs and Veggies

1 to 2 Tbsp. grass-fed butter
2 to 3 organic pastured eggs
Chopped tomatoes
Chopped onions
Chopped peppers
Button mushrooms
Shredded spinach

1 Tbsp. cold-pressed extra-virgin olive oil or avocado oil (optional)
¼ to ½ avocado, sliced (optional)
1 to 2 slices organic cheese (optional)

Melt the butter in a skillet over low heat. Add the eggs and vegetables, and cook until the eggs are softly scrambled. Add the olive oil or avocado oil at the end if using. (Men will usually need 3 Tbsp. of oil per meal, and women 2 to 2 ½ Tbsp. per meal). Place the avocado and cheese on top if desired. Serves 1.

#2—*Eggs and Meat*

2 to 3 organic pastured eggs

Chopped tomatoes

Chopped onions

Chopped peppers

Button mushrooms

Shredded spinach

1 to 2 Tbsp. grass-fed butter

1 to 3 Tbsp. cold-pressed
extra-virgin olive oil or
avocado oil (optional) or
1 to 2 slices organic cheese

2 to 3 oz. cooked ham or
turkey bacon or 2 to 3 slices
cooked nitrite-free bacon

Cook the eggs and veggies in butter as in the previous recipe, and before serving add, if desired, the cheese or the oil (men will usually need 3 Tbsp. of oil per meal, women 2 to 2 ½ Tbsp.). Serve with ham, turkey bacon, or nitrite-free bacon (limit to 1 to 2 times a week). Serves 1.

#3—*Smoked Salmon and Avocado*

1 small avocado, cut into
wedges

Himalayan salt

2 to 4 oz. smoked salmon
slices

Wrap the avocado wedges with salmon slices. Season with Himalayan salt. (As an alternate, you can turn this into a sandwich by placing the avocado and smoked salmon, along with sliced tomatoes, sliced onions, and black pepper, on 1 to 2 pieces of seed bread.) Serves 1.

> ## IT'S A FACT
>
> It is best to use olive oil as a dressing or to add it after cooking. Heating the olive oil causes oxidation, which you do not want.

#4—*Pumpkin Pancakes*

Pancakes:

1 cup pumpkin purée

1 cup cream cheese

1 cup coconut flour

3 organic pastured eggs

2 Tbsp. stevia

¼ cup melted grass-fed butter

½ tsp. pumpkin pie spice

Coconut oil or grass-fed butter

Syrup:

1 cup raspberries or strawberries

4 Tbsp. grass-fed butter

Mix the pumpkin, cream cheese, coconut flour, eggs, stevia, melted grass-fed butter, and pumpkin pie spice together in a bowl, and let stand for 20 minutes. Heat the coconut oil or grass-fed butter in a skillet over medium-heat. When hot, spoon the batter into the pan. Cook until small bubbles form on the top. Flip and cook until the second side is brown.

Make a syrup by simmering the berries with grass-fed butter until the berries begin to release their juices. Makes about 10 pancakes.

#5—*Berry Smoothie*

6 to 8 oz. low-sugar almond or coconut milk

1 Tbsp. almond butter, macadamia nut butter, or pecan butter

1 scoop egg white protein or 1 Tbsp. hydrolyzed

grass-fed collagen protein or 1 scoop fermented plant protein

1 Tbsp. MCT oil powder or coconut oil

¼ tsp. stevia

¼ cup frozen berries

Place all the ingredients in a blender, and process until smooth. If you use fresh berries instead of frozen, add a few ice cubes at the end, and process until the ice is crushed. Serves 1.

#6—Chocolate Smoothie
This smoothie tastes like a chocolate and peanut butter dessert.

6 to 8 oz. low-sugar almond or coconut milk

1 tsp. unsweetened cocoa powder

¼ to ½ tsp. stevia

1 scoop protein powder

1 Tbsp. almond butter, organic peanut butter, or macadamia nut butter

1 Tbsp. MCT oil powder or oil

Place all the ingredients in a blender, and process until smooth. Add ice to desired thickness. Serves 1.

#7—Coconut and Walnut Cereal
Serve this cereal with unsweetened almond milk or coconut milk. Store remaining cereal in a resealable bag and keep in fridge.

3 cups unsweetened shaved coconut

1 cup finely chopped walnuts

1 Tbsp. vanilla extract

½ tsp. stevia

1 Tbsp. cinnamon

½ tsp. sea salt or Himalayan salt (optional)

Preheat the oven to 300°F. Place the coconut and walnuts on a rimmed baking sheet. Sprinkle with the vanilla and stir. Bake until lightly browned. Remove from the oven, and sprinkle with the stevia, cinnamon, and salt if using. Stir until well mixed. Serving size: ½ to 1 cup.

#9—Keto Zone Coffee

¾ to 1 cup brewed hot
coffee (ideally
single-source)

1 Tbsp. MCT oil powder

¼ tsp. stevia

1 Tbsp. avocado oil or grass-
fed butter

½ to 1 tsp. unsweetened
cocoa powder (optional)

Place all the ingredients in a blender, and process until smooth and thick. Alternately, you can briskly stir the oil, butter, stevia, and cocoa powder, if using, into a cup of hot coffee. Serves 1.

LUNCHES

#1—Salad with Protein

Salad:

3 to 6 oz. cooked chicken,
steak, turkey, or salmon
(3 to 4 oz. for women,
4 to 6 oz. for men)

Romaine lettuce or arugula
or field greens or spinach

Cucumbers

Tomatoes

Celery

3 to 4 Tbsp. Oil and Vinegar
Dressing (see recipe below)
or store-bought oil and
vinegar dressing made
without soybean oil

Shredded organic cheese
(rotate cheese every 3 days)

Pile salad greens and vegetables in a salad bowl or plate. Add cooked protein, cut into strips. Add dressing and cheese, if using. Serves 1.

Oil and Vinegar Dressing:

¼ cup apple cider vinegar

¾ cup cold-pressed extra-
   virgin olive oil or
   avocado oil

Onion juice to taste

Garlic juice to taste

Oregano to taste

Salt and pepper to taste

Whisk together the oil and vinegar in a small bowl, or place in a glass jar with a tight-fitting lid and shake until blended. Add the onion juice, garlic juice, oregano, salt, and pepper, and whisk or shake again. You usually need 3 to 4 Tbsp. of dressing on a salad. Makes about 1 cup.

#2—Chicken Salad

3 to 4 Tbsp. olive oil–based
   mayo or avocado oil mayo
   from a health food store
   (without soybean or
   canola oil)

Chopped celery

Chopped onions

Chopped nonsweet pickles

Jalapeño cream cheese

3 to 6 oz. boiled or rotisserie
   chicken, chopped or
   shredded (3 to 4 oz. for
   women, 4 to 6 oz. for men)

Salt and pepper and other
   spices, to taste

Combine all the ingredients in a medium bowl, and toss to mix well. Serve plain or with a green salad or on seed bread. Serves 1. (Mayonnaise usually only contains 10 grams of fat per tablespoon, and olive oil contains 13.5 grams of fat per tablespoon.)

IT'S A FACT

The fridge is the best place to store nuts, to prevent mold and rubbery texture.

#3—*Tongol Tuna Salad*

3 to 4 Tbsp. olive oil–based mayo or avocado oil mayo

Pecans, almonds, or walnuts

Tomato

Avocado

Lettuce

Chopped onion

Chopped celery

1 (5-oz.) can Tongol tuna packed in water (low-mercury tuna), drained

Chive or jalapeño cream cheese (optional)

Combine all ingredients in a medium bowl. Eat plain, on lettuce leaves, or on seed bread. Serves 1.

#4—*Chicken and Vegetable Soup*

Use any veggies you like (broccoli, green beans, cabbage, celery, onion, peppers, garlic, mushrooms, spinach, tomato, collard greens, and kale) as long as they are nonstarchy. Store leftovers in the fridge. If light-headed during the day, this soup will usually help a lot.

1 (3- to 4-lb.) free-range chicken, skin removed

Organic chicken stock (enough to cover the chicken)

Sliced garlic

Sliced onions

Chopped celery

Green beans

Mushrooms

Chopped broccoli

2 to 3 Tbsp. cold-pressed extra-virgin olive oil (or 1 ½ Tbsp. olive oil and 1 ½ Tbsp. grass-fed butter)

Himalayan salt

Chopped cilantro (optional)

Combine the chicken, chicken stock, garlic, and onions in a slow cooker. Cook on low for a few hours. (Alternately cook in a large pot on the stovetop. Bring to a boil and cook for 1 hour and 15 minutes, and then reduce the heat to low and simmer.) Add the remaining vegetables, oil, and salt 15 minutes before serving so veggies are not mushy. To serve, pull chicken apart, and place pieces in soup bowls. Ladle broth and vegetables on top. Top with chopped cilantro, if using. To save cooking time, you can also cut the chicken into pieces and boil for 30 to 40 minutes.

#5—Hamburger Wrap
Serve this burger wrap with a side salad topped with nuts and avocado (if desired) and Oil and Vinegar Dressing (recipe on page 201).

3 to 6 oz. grass-fed hamburger, cooked (3 to 4 oz. for women, 4 to 6 oz. for men)
Romaine lettuce leaves
Sliced tomato
Sliced onion

Mustard
2 Tbsp. olive oil-based mayo or avocado oil mayo
Avocado slices (optional)
1 to 2 (½-ounce) slices organic cheese (optional)

Place the cooked burger on lettuce leaves and top with remaining ingredients. Serves 1.

IT'S A FACT

How to make your own mayo:
In a small bowl vigorously whisk 1 egg yolk, 1 tsp. Dijon mustard, ¾ cup extra-virgin olive oil, 1 Tbsp. lemon juice, 1 Tbsp. apple cider vinegar, ¼ tsp. salt, and 1 tsp. garlic powder until smooth and emulsified.

#6—Sandwich on Seed Bread

Place chicken salad or tuna salad on seed bread. You may substitute 3 to 6 oz. chicken, turkey, fish, or beef. Add a side salad if desired, with 2 to 3 Tbsp. of the olive oil and apple cider vinegar dressing.

#7—Mozzarella and Tomato Salad

1 ½ cups sliced tomatoes	Cold-pressed extra-virgin
8 to 10 oz. burrata balls	olive oil
(made from mozzarella	Salt and pepper to taste
and cream)	Minced garlic (optional)
¼ cup minced basil leaves	Balsamic vinegar (optional)

Place the tomatoes and cheese on a plate, sprinkle with basil, and drizzle with olive oil. Add salt and pepper, and sprinkle with garlic if using. You may also drizzle with a small amount of balsamic vinegar. Serves 1.

DINNERS

#1—Shrimp Scampi

Serve the scampi with veggies of your choice, such as asparagus, green beans, and broccoli with butter. Add a side salad if desired.

2 Tbsp. grass-fed butter	Juice of ½ lemon
3 to 6 oz. wild (not farm-raised) shrimp, peeled (3 to 4 oz. for women, 4 to 6 oz. for men)	1 to 2 Tbsp. cold-pressed extra-virgin olive oil (optional)
1 garlic clove, minced	Salt and pepper to taste

Heat the butter in a large skillet over medium heat. When melted, add the shrimp, and cook until pink and done throughout, 2 to 3 minutes. Add the garlic, salt, pepper, and lemon juice, and cook 1 minute. Drizzle with olive oil after cooking if using. Serves 1.

#2—Rib Eye Dinner

Grill or roast 3 to 6 oz. grass-fed rib eye (3 to 4 oz. for women, 4 to 6 oz. for men) at low heat until meat is done. May place 1 Tbsp. grass-fed butter on top of the rib eye when it's ready to remove from the grill or oven, or add butter to a side of veggies. Leftover meat can be stored in the fridge for the next day's lunch. Add a side salad. May add ½ to 1 cup of cooked broccoli, topped with 1 to 2 Tbsp. grass-fed butter or 1 to 2 Tbsp. cold-pressed extra-virgin olive oil.

#3—Stir-Fry Dinner

1 to 2 Tbsp. grass-fed butter, ghee, or coconut oil

3 to 6 oz. beef, shrimp, or chicken (3 to 4 oz. for women, 4 to 6 oz. for men)

Chinese veggies (chopped broccoli, green beans, shredded cabbage, chopped bok choy, chopped onion, chopped peppers, minced garlic, sliced mushrooms)

1 to 2 Tbsp. cold-pressed extra-virgin olive oil or avocado oil

Chili garlic sauce

Heat the butter in a large skillet over medium heat. When melted, add the meat and cook until almost done. Add vegetables and cook until tender-crisp. Drizzle olive oil or avocado oil on top before serving. Serve with chili garlic sauce. Serves 1.

#4—Chicken Hot Wings

Grill free-range organic chicken wings (3 to 4 oz. for women, 4 to 6 oz. for men) over low heat until done. Serve with guacamole, Tabasco hot sauce dip, or olive oil–based ranch or blue cheese dressing (2 Tbsp. per serving) and celery sticks for dipping. May add a side salad if desired.

#5—Avocado Salad

1 large avocado (8 to 12 oz.), chopped	2 cups spinach, torn
½ cup chopped tomato	¼ cup basil
2 Tbsp. chopped walnuts	Oil and vinegar dressing (see page 201)
¼ cup crumbled feta cheese	Salt and pepper to taste
1 clove garlic, minced	

Combine all the ingredients in a bowl, and toss well. If you'd like to add extra protein, toss in chunks of cooked fish, shrimp, chicken, or steak (3 to 4 oz. for women, 4 to 6 oz. for men). Serves 1.

#6—Grilled Salmon and Spinach

Salmon:

3 to 6 oz. wild salmon (3 to 4 oz. for women, 4 to 6 oz. for men)	Chili powder
	Salt and pepper to taste
	Juice of ½ lemon
Cold-pressed extra-virgin olive oil	1 to 2 Tbsp. grass-fed butter (optional)
2 garlic cloves, minced, divided	

Spinach:

1 to 2 Tbsp. grass-fed butter

1 (5-oz.) bag of baby spinach

1 to 2 Tbsp. cold-pressed extra-virgin olive oil

To prepare the salmon, brush the salmon with the olive oil, and scatter half of the minced garlic on top. Sprinkle with the chili powder, salt, and pepper. Grill over medium heat until fish flakes easily with a fork. Remove from heat, and drizzle with the lemon juice. If desired, place butter on top of salmon.

To prepare the spinach, heat the butter in a large skillet over medium heat. Add the spinach, and cook until slightly wilted. Add the remaining garlic, and cook 1 minute more. Drizzle the olive oil over the spinach before serving. Serves 1.

SNACKS

#1—Chocolate

Dark chocolate (85% or higher cacao): Eat 2 to 3 squares (about ¼ of a bar), daily if desired. I enjoy 1 to 2 squares of Ghirardelli Intense Dark chocolate squares (86% cacao).

#2—Trail Mix

Nuts (macadamia, pecans, almonds, walnuts), small pieces of 85% or higher cacao dark chocolate, and sugar-free coconut flakes. Store in bags in the fridge. A handful at a time is a good portion.

> **IT'S A FACT**
>
> Men generally need 3 to 3½ Tbsp. of fats per meal and women need 2 to 2 ½ Tbsp. of fats per meal. If you eat too much, weight loss is slower.

#3—Celery with Dip

Serve celery sticks with guacamole, salsa, cream cheese (with jalapeño or chives), or nut butters.

#4—Homemade Seed Bread

3 Tbsp. ground chia seeds

3 Tbsp. ground psyllium seeds

¾ cup raw sunflower seeds

¾ cup ground flaxseeds

1 cup ground hemp seeds

¾ cup ground pumpkin seeds

1 tsp. salt

½ tsp. stevia (1 packet)

1 ½ cups water

1 ½ Tbsp. coconut oil, melted

1 ½ Tbsp. ghee, melted

Combine all the seeds, salt, and stevia in a large bowl, and mix well. In a small bowl mix together the water, coconut oil, and ghee. Pour the water mixture over the seed mixture, stir well, and then let stand 2 to 3 hours. Preheat the oven to 350°F. Line a loaf pan with parchment paper. Pour the batter into the pan, and bake 20 minutes. Rotate the pan and bake an additional 50 to 60 minutes.

DESSERTS

#1—Frozen Lemon Pudding

½ cup lemon juice

1 to 2 tsp. stevia (equivalent of 1 cup confectionery sugar)

4 pastured organic eggs

½ cup (1 stick) grass-fed butter

2 tsp. unflavored grass-fed powdered gelatin

Combine all the ingredients in a saucepan. Heat over low heat until just before the mixture comes to a boil. (Do not boil.) Let cool slightly, and then pour into smaller containers or ice cube trays, and freeze. Eat like ice cream in ½ cup servings.

#2—Fudgy Brownies

Brownies:

½ cup (1 stick) grass-fed butter, melted

1 to 2 tsp. stevia (equivalent of 1 cup confectionery sugar)

1 cup unsweetened cocoa powder

4 pastured organic eggs

1 tsp. vanilla extract

¼ tsp. sea salt

Frosting:

6 Tbsp. grass-fed butter, softened

½ to 1 tsp. stevia (1 to 2 packets)

1 tsp. vanilla extract

⅓ cup unsweetened cocoa powder

¼ cup organic heavy cream

Sea salt (optional)

Grass-fed butter

To prepare the brownies, preheat the oven to 325°F. Line an 8-inch square pan with parchment paper, and butter the paper with grass-fed butter. Combine all the ingredients in a large bowl, and whisk until smooth. Pour the batter into the pan, and bake 20 minutes.

To prepare the frosting, beat the butter, stevia, and cocoa together with a hand held electric mixer at medium speed until blended. Add the cream a little at a time, and continue beating until smooth and spreadable. Beat in the vanilla. Spread on top of the brownies in the pan. Sprinkle the frosting with the sea salt if using. Cut into 9 squares.

#3—*Chocolate Butter Balls*

½ cup grass-fed butter

¼ cup coconut oil

½ cup coconut butter

3 Tbsp. unsweetened cocoa
powder

½ to 1 tsp. stevia

Combine all ingredients in a blender, and process until smooth. Spoon into 1-inch balls and place in fridge to cool.

#4—*Chocolate Whip*

1 Tbsp. unsweetened cocoa
powder

1 tsp. stevia (2 packets)

4 oz. organic heavy cream

1 Tbsp. almond butter

1 Tbsp. MCT oil powder

Combine all ingredients in a blender, and process until smooth. Scrape into a bowl or freezer container. Cover. Chill or freeze. (Later, when you reach your goal weight, you can add ½ cup of Halo Top vanilla bean ice cream, which contains 8 g. of carbs per serving.)

BEVERAGES

Drink about 8 ounces of water several times each day. Alkaline, spring water, filtered water, or sparkling water are the best options. Water with a lemon or lime wedge is nice, with a squirt of liquid stevia or monk fruit (lo han guo) if you want.

Other beverages include coffee, green tea, black tea, and a few select unsweetened nut milks (almond milk and coconut milk). Keto Zone Coffee with MCT oil powder and grass-fed butter or avocado oil is one of my favorites. Adding dark cocoa powder (1 tsp.) and stevia (½ tsp.) is a nice option as well.

Make sure to avoid beverages with artificial sweeteners or even natural sugars. They will bump you out of the Keto Zone.

A dairy alternative in any drink or recipe can be coconut cream, which is thicker, richer, and sweeter than coconut milk. The cream that rises to the top of a can of coconut milk is the coconut cream.

Let everything you eat and drink keep you right where you want to be—in the middle of the Keto Zone.

"With my KCL number in hand,
I feel in control of my life
and my weight."
—*Dawn*

CHAPTER SIXTEEN

DISCOVER YOUR KCL NUMBER TO MAINTAIN YOUR IDEAL WEIGHT

LISA NEEDED TO LOSE about thirty pounds, but she wanted to shed an additional ten to fifteen pounds after that. She had her *need* goal and then her *dream* goal. I think she was more motivated by her dream goals, but if she achieved those, all her need goals would be met as well.

Almost forty-five years old, with a waist of thirty-nine inches, she knew from our discussions that she was both carbohydrate sensitive and insulin resistant. I was guessing metabolic syndrome or pre-diabetes were also knocking at her door, but her lab results were pending. I was confident the Keto Zone diet would correct those without addressing them at the start.

"I have been wondering why my weight keeps steadily increasing no matter what I do, so this makes great sense," she explained. "My husband and I are clearing out the pantry and then going shopping this weekend."

The fact that she understood what her body was doing and what it needed gave her great comfort and peace of mind. The actual food ratio of 70 percent fats with 15 percent proteins and 15 percent green veggie carbs was new to her, but she took it all in stride. She was more than ready to begin.

A few months later, Lisa and her husband dropped by my office. They both looked great. I guessed she was close to accomplishing her first goal.

"Together we have lost almost fifty pounds," she stated emphatically. "But we have a question that we have not been able to figure out."

"Okay," I answered. "You are both doing well and have mastered the weight-loss process. How can I help?"

"When we started out we were super diligent in keeping the carb intake each day to 20 grams or less," she explained. "As the weight came off, about two months into it, we relaxed a bit with the diet and ate some more of the healthy foods that contained more carbs, and that pushed us above the 20 grams per day. We are still losing weight, yet we are both eating about 50 grams of carbs per day."

"Is the rate of weight loss slowing down?" I asked.

"Yes, it is," her husband said. "I was losing about two pounds a week when we started, and I would say I'm losing about half a pound a week now."

"The same for me," Lisa added.

"Then you are very close to your Keto Carb Limit (KCL) number," I explained. "I'm guessing your KCL is around 75 grams per day. When you reach that number, whatever it turns out to be, and weight loss stops, remember that

---

IT'S A FACT

In three days you are usually in the Keto Zone, but it may take months to shake loose the desire for junk food.

number. Eating above that number will usually mean weight gain and below it will usually mean weight loss. Congratulations! You have found your KCL."

THE POWER OF KNOWING YOUR KCL

Weight loss is maximized at the low carb amount of 20 grams per day. Even though Lisa and her husband were losing weight by eating 50 grams of carbs per day, the speed of weight loss at 20 grams was much greater.

One beautiful thing about our bodies is that we all have our own built-in number that is the threshold around which we can create the life we want. The healthier we become, such as resensitizing our bodies to carbohydrates and decreasing insulin resistance, usually the higher our number will be.

Specifically, your KCL number is typically the result of several factors, including:

- Foods you have eaten to this point
- Current health and weight
- Age
- Level of exercise
- Genetic history
- Hormonal issues
- Gender
- Medications

Your KCL number will inch up a little as you lose weight and your overall health improves. Another big factor is exercise and medications, but you cannot do anything about some of the other factors.

When you know your KCL, be it 50, 75, or 100 grams, you know exactly how your body is wired. You can plan your meals and adjust things as needed, all while your weight is exactly where you want it to be.

Your KCL is your secret combination. It is your number to health, balanced appetite hormones, and weight that is under your control. It is your number that controls all the other numbers, such as your LDL, HDL, and triglyceride numbers.

Knowledge is power, especially when it comes to your KCL number. Not only do you have power over your weight, but you have peace of mind as well. You know exactly what is needed to lose weight, anytime you want. You are in control!

Any obstacles related to weight that may have been in your path before are now gone. A healthy lifestyle, and all that it brings with it, from the top of your head to the bottom of your feet, is now yours.

Basically, your KCL number is your ticket to the life you want.

HOW TO FIND YOUR KCL

Finding your KCL is easy. In fact, you will usually find it by accident whether you are looking for it or not.

The Keto Zone diet starts at 20 grams of carbs per day on purpose because it is a number far below what most people need in order to lose weight. Starting out at 20 grams of carbs is ideal because of what it means for you, which includes:

- Faster weight loss
- Faster entry into the Keto Zone
- Faster cleaning out of the system
- Faster path to health
- Faster speed to accomplish your goals

After four to eight weeks in the Keto Zone, your KCL number is ready to be revealed. You might not know what it is this very instant, but it should be stable enough that you can identify it.

You have been at 20 grams of carbs while regularly losing weight. To find your Keto Carb Limit (KCL) number, begin to increase your daily carb intake by 10 grams each week. (If you want to continue losing weight, stay at the 20 grams a day carb intake amount until you have lost all the weight you want, then raise your carbs each week by 10 grams to find your KCL.) Add hummus, some beans, and some fruit to reach your KCL number rather than adding grains, potatoes, or excessive dairy. If cheese does not negatively affect you, then you can use cheese.

> ### IT'S A FACT
> If you introduce all the carbs back that you once ate, you will eventually gain all the weight back.

At the same time, keep a careful watch on your ketones.

With this slow increase in carb intake, you will still lose weight, but much more slowly, and you will be able to discern the most accurate reading of your KCL number.

During this process, you will have been in the Keto Zone beyond the month long window in which the urine strips can measure your ketone levels. For accurate ketone readings at this point, you will need to use the ketone breath analyzer or a blood ketone monitor. Some people try to guess based on symptoms, such as whether their weight loss has ceased, and though that is fairly accurate, measuring your ketone levels will help you be sure of what your number is.

As your carbs increase, you will notice your ketone levels decrease a little bit the first few weeks. Then after increasing daily carbs by 10 grams for a couple weeks, you will reach a point where the ketones are down to 0. Weight loss stopped.

Congratulations! You have found your KCL (Keto Carb Limit) number.

Once you have your KCL number in hand, since you are still working to lose weight, dial your carb intake back to 20 grams per day. You will see your ketones jump back to 0.5 to 5 millimolars, and you will be deep within the Keto Zone again, burning fat as fast and furiously as before.

WHAT NEXT?

Knowing your KCL number is quite an accomplishment. It has been the elusive number that has controlled every weight-loss plan you have undertaken. It has also played a significant part in every exercise plan and all the New Year's resolutions to eat healthy you have started.

Up until this moment, it has controlled you, but now the tables have turned. That mysterious number is now known. It is your KCL number, and that means the end of all outside or unknown controls. You are the one in charge. You have the control.

Armed with your KCL number, I suggest that you keep going with the Keto Zone diet until you have achieved your ideal weight.

Maybe you are wondering, *How long can I stay in the Keto Zone?*

The answer is easy enough: stay in the Keto Zone for as long as you want.

Stay deep in the Keto Zone until you have burned off all the extra fat and you are at your desired weight goal. At that point, you basically have three choices to consider:

1. Stay in a mild ketosis state—healthy, all the benefits of the Keto Zone, and weight control.
2. Transfer to an anti-inflammatory diet—more healthy food options, and with knowledge of your KCL, you'll be able to control your weight. (See the diet outlined in my book *Let Food Be Your Medicine*.)
3. Go back to eating what you used to eat—this will most likely result in your gaining back the weight you lost, not to mention the adverse health effects.

Based on everything you have learned up to this point, you would not recommend the third option to anyone. Neither would I.

The second option is a great one, healthy, and definitely a viable long-term health plan that enables you to maintain your weight while having a lot more food options. Your KCL number will be a very useful tool to help you manage the healthy carbs (brown rice, sweet potatoes, beans, peas, lentils, and hummus with their lower glycemic index, which means less insulin) that you eat on this anti-inflammatory diet. I recommend it to many, especially to young people, families, and growing teens who need a small amount of healthy carbs. You can always swing back to the Keto Zone diet; the return trip from here would be smooth enough.

> ### IT'S A FACT
>
> After you achieve your goal weight, eat carbs and starches in small amounts (about the size of a tennis ball) at night. It will usually improve your sleep by boosting serotonin levels.

The first option, staying in a mild ketosis state, is the healthiest option of all. One of my patients, a sweet sixty-year-old grandmother, came to me with advanced stage-4 metastatic breast cancer that had also metastasized to her ribs, sternum, and spine. With that diagnosis, you usually only have a short time to live.

That was more than two years ago! She immediately went on the Keto Zone diet, and though the Keto Zone diet is not a cure for all diseases, it has without question been the cornerstone to her health. Her PET scans are now showing no active disease. About the Keto Zone diet, she is quick to exclaim, "This is the easiest dietary program I have ever followed. I am so satisfied. I will always eat this way." I would guess that she has many years ahead of her, much to her and her grandkids' delight.

Staying in the Keto Zone, right at the edge of what is a very mild state of ketosis, is also the place that gives you the greatest control over your weight.

THREE STEPS TO STAYING IN THE KETO ZONE OVER THE LONG TERM

Thankfully, you can hold on to all those incredible benefits you have found in the Keto Zone. You can continue to live life with the same limitless energy, youthfulness, alertness, memory, focus, and zest for life. All of this is, of course, without food cravings and raging appetite hormones.

Staying in the Keto Zone over the long term is an easy three-step process:

STEP 1—RETURN TO YOUR KCL NUMBER

Whatever your KCL number, increase your carb intake until you have reached that amount. For most people, it is a number between 50 and 100 grams of carbs per day.

Increase your carbs by adding other healthy foods, such as beans, peas, hummus, lentils, seeds, nuts, cheese, full-fat yogurt, and low glycemic fruits that have sufficient carbs to reach your KCL number. Not too much, just enough. (See appendix B for a list of healthy carbs that you can use to find your KCL.)

STEP 2—AIM JUST BELOW YOUR KCL NUMBER

You want to stay at a point just below your KCL number. Find your number, then back it up a bit. If you find that 75 grams of carbs per day is your KCL number, then set 70 grams as your new target number. This is your long-term number that will enable you to stay in the Keto Zone and enjoy all the benefits you have come to love so much.

> ### IT'S A FACT
> Every step forward is a step in the right direction.

Technically, this is a mild state of ketosis. You are hovering just inside the Keto Zone. Exceed the daily carb limit, and you will probably bump yourself out of the Keto Zone, but keep the carbs limited, and you will remain in the Keto Zone. It is a balance, but you will be a master of it in no time.

When you reach your goal weight, I recommend that you weigh yourself daily. If your weight starts to slowly increase, it is time to get below your KCL number to get the weight off.

STEP 3—LIVE LIFE AS YOU CHOOSE

Not only will you achieve your weight-loss goals, but you will have a proven system that positively impacts your life in countless other ways as well. After all, maintaining your good health is so much easier when you are at your ideal weight.

Life is different at this point. Every single health benefit of the

Keto Zone is yours to keep. Imagine being able to virtually close the door on almost every preventable disease, almost every obesity-related disease, almost all heart disease issues, countless inflammatory diseases, and a host of other ailments.

Maybe you have reversed type 2 diabetes, early dementia, fatty liver, or an autoimmune disease. You have a pretty good reason to stick to the Keto Zone diet.

On top of it, you love how you feel. It is a sweet spot. Your mind is clear, you have boundless energy, and you feel good.

The entire Keto Zone diet is balanced, healthy, and ideal for weight loss, health, and longevity. It is admittedly pretty incredible. That is quite a lifestyle you have there.

CONCLUSION

A FEW THINGS CONCLUDE at this point, such as yo-yo diet methods, trying to lose weight while still living on a high-carb diet, and having to worry about the latest diet trends.

You could also say that fat phobia concludes as well, along with the fear of egg yolks causing heart disease and drugs being the only answer to lowering LDL cholesterol.

Ending as well are the late-night bowls of ice cream and afternoon sugar fixes, but based on what you now know, that is a good thing.

Let end what needs to end so you can grab hold of your new beginning.

If you want to burn off any excess weight, you know exactly how. It is no longer a mystery, nor is it a painful process.

If you have a disease that the Keto Zone can treat, prevent, or manage, now you have an answer. You have hope.

Basically, you are free to focus on building the future of your choosing.

You are free.

Now enjoy!

ONE LAST WORD
FOR THOSE OVER THIRTY

IF YOU ARE OVER THIRTY YEARS OLD and were unable to reach your goal on the Keto Zone diet, please get your sex hormones and thyroid hormones checked and balanced by a doctor well trained in bioidentical hormone replacement. I prefer hormone pellets of estrogen and testosterone instead of pills, shots, and creams. To find a medical doctor trained in bioidentical replacement hormone pellets, go to www.bioTEmedical.com.

APPENDICES

Appendix A

SUPPLEMENTS

Depending on your health and your sickness, one or more supplements may help speed you along the trail toward health. To review the supplements beforehand, go to www.drcolbert.com. You can order at any time.

Divine Health Nutritional Products
Shop.drcolbert.com
407-732-6952

- Green Supremefood: a whole food nutritional powder with fermented grasses and vegetables
- Red Supremefood: a whole food nutritional powder with antiaging fruits
- Fermented protein superfood
- Enhanced multivitamin
- Living krill oil
- MCT oil capsules
- MCT oil powder
- Ketosis strips
- Living enzyme
- Living probiotic
- Living hydrolyzed collagen

HEALTHY CARBS FOR FINDING YOUR KCL

After you have reached your ideal weight, it is time to slowly increase your daily carb intake from the Keto Zone's starting point of
20 grams per day. At the start of each week, increase your daily carb
intake by a total of 10 grams. After a week at 30 grams of carbs per
day, increase to 40 grams for the next week, and so on. When you
get to the point where you are neither gaining nor losing weight,
you are at your KCL, your Keto Carb Limit.

These healthy carbs are great to use as you increase your carb
intake in 10-gram increments:

- Beans, cooked (kidney, lima, navy, pinto, white, lentils, or
  brown): ¼ cup, 10 g. carbs
- Peas: raw ½ cup, 10 g. carbs
- Hummus: 4 Tbsp., 10 g. carbs
- Seeds:
  - Chia seeds: 3 Tbsp., 12 g. carbs
  - Flax seeds: 3 Tbsp., 9 g. carbs
  - Pumpkin seeds: ½ cup, 15 g. carbs
  - Sunflower seeds: ¼ cup, 7 g. carbs
- Nuts, dry or roasted:
  - Almonds: ½ cup, 13 g. carbs
  - Cashews: ¼ cup, 10 g. carbs
  - Peanuts: ¼ cup, 7.5 g. carbs
  - Pecans: ½ cup, 7 g. carbs

- Cream cheese (regular): 8 oz., 9 g. carbs
- Full-fat yogurt: 8 oz., 10 g. carbs
- Low glycemic fruits
  - Apples: ½ medium apple, 9 g. of carbs
  - Blueberries: ½ cup, 10 g. carbs
  - Raspberries: ½ cup, 9 g. carbs
  - Strawberries: 1 cup, 12 g. carbs

Appendix C

FOR ADVANCED-CANCER PATIENTS

For advanced-cancer patients, including patients with autoimmune diseases (who do not respond to the regular ketogenic diet), focus on decreasing inflammatory foods, because inflammation fuels cancer. Of the foods in the Keto Zone diet, veggies and fats will not cause inflammation (unless the patient happens to be allergic). That leaves the protein foods.

Specifically with proteins, processed meats such as pepperoni, ham, hotdogs, bologna, sausage, salami, and even bacon are known to cause cancer. Some argue that red meats in general cause cancer, but that has not been verified.

Therefore, in an effort to maximize your fight against cancer while keeping your body in the Keto Zone, I suggest the following:

- Maintain the usual consumption of veggies
- Maintain the usual consumption of fats
- Adjust protein intake
  - Remove all processed meats
  - Lower protein intake moderately (instead of 4 to 6 oz. per meal for men, eat 2 to 4 oz.; for women, instead of 3 to 4 oz. per meal, eat 2 to 3 oz.)

For advanced-cancer patients, decreasing inflammatory foods is vitally important. Protein is still a necessary part of your diet, so choose only foods that are wild, organic, and free range. For now, all processed meats need to go.

The standard American diet is full of animal protein, which is a major source of arachidonic acid (an omega-6 fat that can increase inflammation dramatically). Arachidonic acid produces many powerful inflammatory mediators, including leukotrienes, thromboxanes, prostaglandins, and prostacyclins. Patients with advanced cancers such as stage 3 and stage 4 cancers should limit foods high in arachidonic acid. These foods include:

1. Red meat (especially fatty cuts of red meat)
2. White meat (chicken, duck, and wild fowl)
3. Dairy (any milk or yogurt)
4. Eggs (the yolk and not the white, or 1 yolk with 3 egg whites is okay)
5. Cheese (specifically hard cheese since soft cheeses typically have less arachidonic acid)
6. Certain fish (catfish, tilapia and yellowtail)[84]

According to the 2005–6 National Health and Nutrition Examination Survey, these foods are the top contributors of arachidonic acid in the American diet:

#1. White meats (chicken)
#2. Eggs
#3. Beef/beef products
#4. Sausage, franks, bacon, and ribs
#5. Other fish/fish dishes
#6. Burgers
#7. Cold cuts
#8. Pork/pork-mixed dishes

#9. Mexican mixed dishes

#10. Pizza (#10)[85]

Dr. Thomas Seyfried, who has done considerable diet research on mice, has found that a ketogenic diet slows down stage 3 and stage 4 advanced cancers. For stage 3 and stage 4 cancer patients, I recommend that they decrease animal proteins to about 5 to 10 percent of their total calories and increase their fat from the standard 70 percent to 80 percent of their total calories. Also, I suggest keeping green veggies and salad veggies at about 10 to 15 percent of total calories.

Decades ago, Dr. T. Colin Campbell conducted studies that showed how a high animal protein diet increased cancer with his lab rats, but when he placed them on a low animal protein diet, the cancers decreased significantly in size. For more information, refer to my book *Let Food Be Your Medicine*.

Appendix D

FOR HIGH-CHOLESTEROL PATIENTS

If your cholesterol goes up, for any reason, most doctors will demand that you stop whatever it is that you are doing. Despite the fact that the Keto Zone diet is healthy (which it is) and you are losing weight (which you should be), they will urge you to stop immediately.

Recall in chapter 6 that there are two forms of LDL cholesterol: pattern A (neutral) and pattern B (plaque forming). The ketogenic diet may raise pattern A, but it usually lowers pattern B.

For me, my total cholesterol is usually around 150, my LDL cholesterol is around 90, and my good HDL is around 55. After six months on the Keto Zone diet, I checked my cholesterol numbers and found that my HDL had increased from 55 to 85, which is an amazing jump!

My total cholesterol went from 150 to 260, and my LDL increased from around 90 to 160. I took the Lipoprofile test to see how the LDL measured with both the neutral pattern A LDL and the bad pattern B LDL. It turns out that the increase was in the pattern A, the neutral LDL, and the bad pattern B LDL was low. Still, I wanted to lower my LDL because it could have affected my insurance rates.

If you have high cholesterol and you notice your cholesterol increasing (as I did), or you just want to make sure your cholesterol numbers do not go up while on the Keto Zone diet, then I suggest the following revision to the previously outlined Keto Zone diet:

- Maintain the usual consumption of veggies
- Maintain the usual consumption of proteins, but minimize or avoid processed meats (bacon, sausage, etc.)
- Adjust fat intake
  - Instead of a 50/50 ratio of saturated fats with monounsaturated fats, change that ratio to 20/80
  - Reduce saturated fats (coconut oil, palm oil, grass-fed butter) to 20% of daily intake or about 2 Tbsp. a day
  - Remove the skins from chicken and limit red meat to 3–6 oz. every other day
  - Limit cheese to 1 or 2 oz. per day
  - Increase monounsaturated fats such as olive oil, avocado oil, almond oil, almond butter, nuts (pecans, almonds, macadamia nuts, etc.), and nut oils to 80% of daily intake
  - Continue to use MCT oil powder or oil and dark cocoa, as they do not raise LDL cholesterol but do raise HDL cholesterol (Japanese researchers found that men who drank cocoa were more resistant to oxidation of LDL cholesterol.[86])
  - Take 1 Tbsp. chia seeds or psyllium seeds one to two times per day
  - Take citrus bergamot supplements (500 mg. two times per day) and/or plant sterols with each meal if needed to lower cholesterol

For most people on the Keto Zone diet, their LDL will usually decrease (the bad pattern B specifically) and their good HDL will usually increase. Both are very good indicators. But should you need to do more to lower your LDL and boost your HDL, following this slightly revised Keto Zone diet, with 20/80 saturated to mono-unsaturated fat, will certainly help. (Please refer to chapter 6 for more information.)

Now, for me, my increased LDL may have affected my insurance rates, but after switching to the 20/80 ratio of saturated to monounsaturated fats, my HDL stayed high at 85 and my LDL decreased from 160 to 110. Not too bad, and my insurance rates did not increase.

If you need to lower your cholesterol numbers, for whatever the reason, my suggestion is that you first lose the weight you want to lose on the Keto Zone diet, then shift to the 20/80 ratio of fats. This will help adjust your cholesterol numbers, should they need adjusting. Remember, the fatty acid composition of our cells is 55 percent monounsaturated fats and only 27 percent saturated fats.

FOR AUTOIMMUNE DISEASE PATIENTS

Please refer to my prior book, Let Food Be Your Medicine, *and read chapter 7 for more information and encouragement on beating autoimmune disease.*

The two main foods that fuel most autoimmune diseases are gluten (mainly from wheat) and dairy. The milk from a cow contains proteins that are different from those found in breast milk. A person with autoimmune disease almost always has impaired intestinal permeability (leaky gut) and usually forms antibodies to dairy proteins. However, these proteins are not present in grass-fed ghee, which is clarified butter. If you have an autoimmune disease, stop all gluten forever and stop dairy containing milk proteins. Grass-fed butter contains only 0.1 grams of dairy proteins per tablespoon, but grass-fed ghee has 0 grams. If you suffer from an autoimmune disease, stop all forms of dairy (except for ghee) for at least six months, and after that *some* patients can introduce a small amount of dairy into their diet every four days. If your symptoms return, stay off all dairy except for ghee.

FOODS TO AVOID

The Keto Zone diet is great for most autoimmune diseases, but the following is a list of potential flare foods that may also need to be eliminated forever, or briefly for six months, or at least limited to every four days.

1. *Nightshades:* Tomatoes, potatoes, paprika, peppers, and eggplant

2. *Genetically modified foods:* Soy, soybean oil, canola oil, corn, corn oil, cottonseed oil, potatoes, papayas, yellow squash, rice, and beets. Approximately 50 percent of the sugar consumed in the United States comes from sugar beets. Notice many of the starches that are to be avoided on the Keto Zone diet (corn, rice, potatoes, squash) are also the main GMO foods consumed by Americans.

3. *Polyunsaturated fats:* Soybean oil, corn oil, safflower oil, sunflower oil, cottonseed oil, grapeseed oil—especially if these oils are heated

4. *Trans fats and fried foods:* This includes all foods fried in monounsaturated and polyunsaturated fats

5. *Sugar:* Remember that approximately 50 percent of the sugar consumed in the United States comes from sugar beets, which are a GMO food. Avoid all sugar on the Keto Zone diet.

6. *Glyphosate:* Foods that contain glyphosate (found in Roundup herbicide) interrupt your gut bacteria's metabolic pathways, which may cause systemic low-grade inflammation. These foods include wheat, oats, soy, corn, lentils, peas, flax, rye, millet, potatoes, beets, sunflowers, and buckwheat. Most of these foods are GMO foods, and also mainly starches. If you eat organic foods, you will avoid glyphosate, which is found in many popular crackers, chips, cereals, and sweetened drinks—all foods to avoid on the Keto Zone diet.

7. *Lectins:* Lectins are carbohydrate-binding proteins that are commonly found in beans, nuts, seeds, and grains. The highest concentration of lectins are found in legumes

(beans, soybeans, peanuts), grains (especially wheat), and nightshades (tomatoes and potatoes). Only about 30 percent of the foods most people eat contain significant amounts of lectins. Lectins can then bind to the lining of the small intestines and damage it, leading to leaky gut. Certain Keto Zone–friendly foods, such as nuts, peanuts, and seeds, may fuel autoimmune disease.

For patients with autoimmune disease, I recommend that they rotate all their foods (except fats) every three to four days. That means not eating the same protein such as chicken every day. Instead, eat chicken one day, turkey the next, followed by fish, and then grass-fed beef before starting the rotation over. This also goes for veggies, fruits, and other foods.

MOST IMPORTANT SUPPLEMENTS FOR AUTOIMMUNE DISEASE

1. *Probiotics:* These help restore the gut. I recommend using one probiotic for three months and then switching to another. My favorite probiotics include Living Probiotic, Beyond Biotics, Florassist GI, Mega Sporebiotic, and Probiophage.
2. *Krill oil and fish oil:* I recommend the krill oil mentioned in appendix A, taking two capsules twice a day. Some patients may also need a quality fish oil.
3. *Vitamin D3:* These help boost your vitamin D level. I recommend 2,000 to 10,000 international units (IU) a day, depending on the results from a 25-OH Vitamin D deficiency blood test.

NOTES

Introduction

1. Michael McCarthy, "US Guideline May Drop Cholesterol Limits but Keep Link Between Dietary Saturated Fats and Trans Fats and Heart Disease," *BMJ* (Feb. 18, 2015), http://www.bmj.com/content/350/bmj.h835.

Chapter One

2. Shivani Garg, "Alzheimer Disease and APOE-4," Medscape (Feb. 1, 2015), http://emedicine.medscape.com/article/1787482-overview.

Chapter Two

3. A. Menotti et al., "Food Intake Patterns and 25-Year Mortality from Coronary Heart Disease: Cross-Cultural Correlations in the Seven Countries Study," abstract, *European Journal of Epidemiology* 15, no. 6 (July 1999): 507–15, https://www.ncbi.nlm.nih.gov/pubmed/10485342.

4. Andreas Eenfeldt, *Low Carb, High Fat Food Revolution* (New York: Skyhorse Publishing, 2014), 37.

5. Mark Hyman, *Eat Fat, Get Thin: Why the Fat We Eat Is the Key to Sustained Weight Loss and Vibrant Health* (New York: Little, Brown and Company, 2016), 14.

6. Nina Teicholz, *The Big Fat Surprise: Why Butter, Meat and Cheese Belong in a Healthy Diet* (New York: Simon & Schuster, 2014), 306.

7. Rajiv Chowdhury et al., "Association of Dietary, Circulating, and Supplement Fatty Acids with Coronary Risk: A Systematic Review and Meta-Analysis," abstract, *Annals of Internal Medicine* 160, no. 6 (March 18, 2014): 398–406, doi: 10.7326/M13-1788, https://www.ncbi.nlm.nih.gov/pubmed/24723079.

Chapter Three

8. Hyman, *Eat Fat, Get Thin*, 4.

9. Joe Leech, "13 Ways That Sugar Soda Is Bad for Your Health," Authority Nutrition, https://authoritynutrition.com/13-ways-sugary-soda-is-bad-for-you/.

10. D. E. Bloom et al., "The Global Economic Burden of Non-Communicable Diseases" (Geneva, Switzerland: World Economic Forum, 2011), 6, http://www3.weforum.org/docs/WEF_Harvard_HE_GlobalEconomicBurdenNonCommunicableDiseases_2011.pdf.

11. William Davis, *Wheat Belly: Lose the Wheat, Lose the Weight, and Find Your Path Back to Health* (New York: Rodale, 2011), 33.

12. Emily A. Hu, "White Rice Consumption and Risk of Type 2 Diabetes: Meta-Analysis and Systematic Review," *BJM* (March 15, 2012), doi: https://doi.org/10.1136/bmj.e1454, http://www.bmj.com/content/344/bmj.e1454.

13. R. B. Ervin and C. L. Ogden, "Consumption of Added Sugars Among U.S. Adults, 2005–2010," NCHS Data Brief, No. 122 (Hyattsville, MD: National Center for Health Statistics, 2013), http://www.cdc.gov/nchs/data/databriefs/db122.pdf.

14. United States Department of Agriculture, Economic Research Service, "USDA Sugar Supply: Tables 51-53: US Consumption of Caloric Sweeteners," http://www.ers.usda.gov/data-products/sugar-and-sweeteners-yearbook-tables.aspx.

15. Hyman, *Eat Fat, Get Thin*, 13.

16. Nora D. Volkow and Ting-Kai Li, "Drug Addiction: The Neurobiology of Behaviour Gone Awry," abstract, *Nature Reviews Neuroscience* 5, no. 12 (Dec. 2004): 963–70, http://www.nature .com/nrn/journal/v5/n12/full/nrn1539.html.

17. Nicole M. Avena, Pedro Rada, and Bartley G. Hoebel, "Evidence for Sugar Addiction: Behavioral and Neurochemical Effects of Intermittent, Excessive Sugar Intake," abstract, *Neuroscience Behavior Review* 32, no. 1 (2008): 20–39, http://www.ncbi.nlm.nih.gov/pubmed /17617461.

18. Alexandra Shapiro et al., "Fructose-Induced Leptin Resistance Exacerbates Weight Gain in Response to Subsequent High-Fat Feeding," abstract, *American Journal of Physiology, Regulatory, Integrative and Comparative Physiology* 295, no. 5 (Nov. 1, 2008): R1370–1375, doi: 10.1152/ajpregu.00195.2008, https://www.ncbi.nlm.nih.gov/pubmed/18703413.

19. Dariush Mozaffarian, Eric B. Rimm, and David M. Herrington, "Dietary Fats, Carbohydrate, and Progression of Coronary Atherosclerosis in Postmenopausal Women," *American Journal of Clinical Nutrition* 80 (2004): 1175–84, http://ajcn.nutrition.org/content/80/5/1175.full.pdf +html.

20. Jeff S. Volek, Matthew J. Sharman, and Cassandra E. Forsythe, "Modification of Lipoproteins by Very Low-Carbohydrate Diets" *Journal of Nutrition* 135, no. 6 (2005): 1339–42, http:// jn.nutrition.org/content/135/6/1339.full.pdf+html.

21. Ronald M. Krauss, "Dietary and Genetic Probes of Atherogenic Dyslipidemia," *Arteriosclerosis, Thrombosis, and Vascular Biology* 25 (2005): 2265–72, http://atvb.ahajournals.org/content /25/11/2265.

22. Chowdhury, "Association of Dietary, Circulating, and Supplement Fatty Acids with Coronary Risk."

23. U.S. Department of Health and Human Services and U.S. Department of Agriculture, *2015– 2020 Dietary Guidelines for Americans*, 8th edition (December 2015), http://health.gov /dietaryguidelines/2015/guidelines/.

Chapter Four

24. To convert your weight to kilograms, multiply your weight in pounds by 0.45359237.

25. A. Paoli et al., "Beyond Weight Loss: A Review of the Therapeutic Uses of Very-Low-Carbohydrate (Ketogenic) Diets," *European Journal of Clinical Nutrition,* 67 (Aug. 2013): 789–96, doi: 10.1038/ejcn.2013.116, http://www.nature.com/ejcn/journal/v67/n8/full /ejcn2013116a.html.

26. Rainer J. Klement and Ulrike Kämmerer, "Is There a Role for Carbohydrate Restriction in the Treatment and Prevention of Cancer?," *Nutrition & Metabolism* 8 (Oct. 26, 2011): 75, doi: 10.1186/1743-7075-8-75, https://nutritionandmetabolism.biomedcentral.com /articles/10.1186/1743-7075-8-75.

27. Gabriela Segura, "The Ketogenic Diet—An Overview," SOTT.net, https://www.sott.net /article/265069-the-ketogenic-diet-an-overview.

28. Chowdhury, "Association of Fatty Acids with Coronary Risk."

29. Jeff Volek and Stephen Phinney, *The Art and Science of Low Carbohydrate Performance* (Miami: Beyond Obesity LLC, 2012), 7.

Chapter Five

30. Eric C. Westman et al., "The Effect of a Low-Carbohydrate, Ketogenic Diet Versus a Low-Glycemic Index Diet on Glycemic Control in Type 2 Diabetes Mellitus," *Nutrition & Metabolism* 5 (2008), doi: 10.1186/1743-7075-5-36, https://nutritionandmetabolism.biomedcentral.com /articles/10.1186/1743-7075-5-36.

Chapter Six

31. Jimmy Moore and Eric Westman, *Cholesterol Clarity: What the HDL Is Wrong with My Numbers?* (Las Vegas, NV: Victory Belt Publishing, 2013), 36.

32. Amanda Gardner, "Most Fast Food French Fries Cooked in Unhealthiest Oil," ABCNews, http://abcnews.go.com/health/healthyday/fast-food-french-fries-cooked-unhealthiest-oils /story?id=9595965.

33. B. V. Howard et al., "Low-Fat Dietary Pattern and Risk of Cardiovascular Disease: The Women's Health Initiative Randomized Controlled Dietary Modification Trial," *Journal of the American Medical Association* 295, no. 6 (Feb. 8, 2006): 655–66, http://jamanetwork.com/journals/jama /fullarticle/202339, doi:10.1001/jama.295.6.655.

34. Lois Baker, "Study Shows Glucose Consumption Increases Production of Destructive Free Radicals, Lowers Level of Key Antioxidant," State University of New York at Buffalo (August 16, 2000), http://www.buffalo.edu/news/releases/2000/08/4839.html.

35. Davis, *Wheat Belly*, 164.

36. Paul Grasgruber et al., "Food Consumption and the Actual Statistics of Cardiovascular Diseases: An Epidemiological Comparison of 42 European Countries," *Food and Nutrition Research* 60, no. 1 (2016), http://www.tandfonline.com/doi/full/10.3402/fnr.v60.31694.

37. Mayo Clinic Staff, "Statin Side Effects: Weigh the Benefits and Risks," Mayo Clinic, www.mayoclinic.org/statin-side-effects/art-20046013.

38. University of Maryland Medical Center, "Coenzyme Q10," http://umm.edu/health/medical /altmed/supplement/coenzyme-q10.

39. Cheol Ung Choi et al., "Statins Do Not Decrease Small, Dense Low-Density Lipoprotein," *Texas Heart Institute Journal* 37, no. 4 (2010): 421–28, https://www.ncbi.nlm.nih.gov/pmc/articles /PMC2929871/.

40. World Health Organization, "Global Health Observatory Data Repository," http://apps.who.int /gho/data/node.main.A865CARDIOVASCULAR?

41. R. J. Wood, "Carbohydrate Restriction Alters Lipoprotein Metabolism by Modifying VLDL, LDL, and HDL Subfraction Distribution and Size in Overweight Men," abstract, *Journal of Nutrition* 136, no. 2 (Feb. 2006): 384–89, https://www.ncbi.nlm.nih.gov/pubmed/16424116.

42. Jeff Volek and Stephen Phinney, *The Art and Science of Low Carbohydrate Living* (Miami, FL: Beyond Obesity, LLC, 2011), 108.

Chapter Seven

43. William Davis, "Wheat and Hunger," WheatBellyBlog.com, http://www.wheatbellyblog.com /2015/08/wheat-makes-you-hungry/.

44. L. C. Hudgins, "Effect of High-Carbohydrate Feeding on Triglyceride and Saturated Fatty Acid Synthesis," abstract, *Proceedings of the Society for Experimental Biology and Medicine* 225, no. 3 (Dec. 2000): 178-83, https://www.ncbi.nlm.nih.gov/pubmed/11082210.

Chapter Eight

45. K. P. Ball et al., "Low-Fat Diet in Myocardial Infarction: A Controlled Trial," *The Lancet* 286, no. 7411 (1965): 501–4; doi: http://dx.doi.org/10.1016/S0140-6736(65)91469-8, https://www.ncbi .nlm.nih.gov/pubmed/4158171.

46. Alberto Ascherio et al., "Dietary Fat and Risk of Coronary Heart Disease in Men: Cohort Follow Up Study in the United States," *BMJ* 313, no. 84 (July 13, 1996), doi: https://doi.org /10.1136/bmj.313.7049.84, http://www.bmj.com/content/313/7049.84.

47. U.S. Department of Health, *2015–2020 Dietary Guidelines*.

48. Glen D. Lawrence, "Dietary Fats and Health: Dietary Recommendations in the Context of

Scientific Evidence," *Advances in Nutrition* 4 (May 2013): 294–302, http://advances.nutrition
.org/content/4/3/294.full.

49. Deborah E. Barnes and Kristine Yaffe, "The Projected Effect of Risk Factor Reduction on
    Alzheimer's Diseases Prevalence," abstract, *The Lancet Neurology* 10, no. 9 (Sept. 2011): 819–28,
    doi: http://dx.doi.org/10.1016/S1474-4422(11)70072-2, http://www.thelancet.com/journals
    /laneur/article/PIIS1474-4422(11)70072-2/abstract/.

50. G. McKellar et al., "A Pilot Study of a Mediterranean-Type Diet Intervention in Female Patients
    with Rheumatoid Arthritis Living in Areas of Social Deprivation in Glasgow," abstract, *Annals
    of Rheumatic Diseases* 66, no. 9 (Sept 2007): 1239–43, doi: 10.1136/ard.2006.065151, https://
    www.ncbi.nlm.nih.gov/pubmed/17613557.

51. "Monounsaturated Fats," American Heart Association, http://www.heart.org/HEARTORG
    /HealthyLiving/HealthyEating/Nutrition/Monounsaturated-Fats_UCM_301460_Article.jsp#
    .WKXjrPJXLm4.

52. Alicja Wolk et al., "A Prospective Study of Association of Monounsaturated Fat and Other
    Types of Fat with Risk of Breast Cancer," *Archives of Internal Medicine* 158, no. 1 (1998): 41–45,
    doi:10.1001/archinte.158.1.41, http://jamanetwork.com/journals/jamainternalmedicine
    /fullarticle/190898.

53. Alex Park, "Five Surprising Things We Feed Cows," *Mother Jones* (Dec. 9, 2013), http://www
    .motherjones.com/blue-marble/2013/12/cow-feed-chicken-poop-candy-sawdust.

54. Edward Group, "Eight Shocking Facts about Bovine Growth Hormone," Global Healing Center
    (Jan. 2, 2014), http://www.globalhealingcenter.com/natural-health/8-shocking-facts-bovine
    -growth-hormone/.

55. A. P. Simopoulos, "The Importance of the Ratio of Omega-6/Omega-3 Essential Fatty Acids,"
    abstract, *Biomedicine & Pharmacotherapy* 56, no. 8 (Oct. 2002): 365–79, https://www.ncbi.nlm
    .nih.gov/pubmed/12442909.

56. Freydis Hjalmarsdottir, "17 Science-Based Benefits of Omega-3 Fatty Acids," Authority
    Nutrition, https://authoritynutrition.com/17-health-benefits-of-omega-3/.

57. Andrew Weil, "Balancing Omega-3 and Omega-6?," (Feb. 22, 2007), https://www.drweil.com
    /vitamins-supplements-herbs/vitamins/balancing-omega-3-and-omega-6/.

58. "Is Margarine Harmful?—6 Secrets They Don't Tell You," Cultured Palate, http://
    myculturedpalate.com/real-foods-info/is-margarine-harmful-6-secrets-they-dont-tell-you/.

59. "FDA Cuts Tans Fats in Processed Foods," U.S. Food and Drug Administrations, http://www.
    fda.gov/ForConsumers/ConsumerUpdates/ucm372915.htm.

60. Meredith Melnick, "How Fake Fakes Can Make You Really Fat," Time.com (June 23, 2001),
    http://healthland.time.com/2011/06/23/study-how-fake-fats-can-make-you-really-fat/.

61. "Interesterified Fats are Deadlier Than Trans Fats," Dr. J, https://medically-no-nonsense.com
    /interesterified-fats-are-deadlier-than-trans-fats/.

Chapter Nine

62. M. McCarthy, "US Guideline May Drop Cholesterol Limits but Keep Link Between Dietary
    Saturated Fats and Trans Fats and Heart Disease," *BMJ* 350 (Feb. 18, 2015), doi: https://doi.org
    /10.1136/bmj.h835, http://www.bmj.com/content/350/bmj.h835.

63. Stacy Simon, "World Health Organization Says Processed Meat Causes Cancer," American
    Cancer Society (Oct. 26, 2015), https://www.cancer.org/latest-news/world-health-organization
    -says-processed-meat-causes-cancer.html.

64. "The Overuse of Antibiotics in Food Animals Threatens Public Health," Consumers Union,
    http://consumersunion.org/news/the-overuse-of-antibiotics-in-food-animals-threatens-public
    -health-2/.

65. Dave Asprey, *The Bulletproof Diet* (New York: Rodale, 2014), 49.

66. J. M. Leheska, "Effects of Conventional and Grass-Feeding Systems on the Nutrient Composition of Beef," abstract, *Journal of Animal Science* 86, no. 12 (Dec. 2008) 3575-85, doi: 10.2527/jas.2007-0565, https://www.ncbi.nlm.nih.gov/pubmed/18641180.

Chapter Ten

67. "Overview of FDA Labeling Requirements for Restaurants, Similar Retail Food Establishments, and Vending Machines," U.S. Food and Drug Administration, https://www.fda.gov/food /ingredientspackaginglabeling/labelingnutrition/ucm248732.htm.

68. A. Shapiro et al., "Fructose-Induced Leptin Resistance Exacerbates Weight Gain in Response to Subsequent High-Fat Feeding," abstract, *American Journal of Physiology—Regulatory, Integrative, and Comparative Physiology* 295, no. 5 (Nov. 2008): R1370–5, doi: 10.1152/ajpregu .00195.2008, https://www.ncbi.nlm.nih.gov/pubmed/18703413.

69. A. A. Gibson et al., "Do Ketogenic Diets Really Suppress Appetite? A Systematic Review and Meta-Analysis," abstract, *Obesity Reviews* 16, no. 1 (Jan. 2015): 64–76, doi: 10.1111/obr.12230, http://www.ncbi.nlm.nih.gov/pubmed/25402637.

70. Jimmy Moore and Eric Westman, *Keto Clarity: Your Definitive Guide to the Benefits of a Low-Carb, High-Fat Diet* (Nevada: Victory Belt Publishing, 2014), 117.

71. A. Ramel et al., "Beneficial Effects of Long-Chain N-3 Fatty Acids Included in an Energy-Restricted Diet on Insulin Resistance in Overweight and Obese European Young Adults," abstract, *Diabetologia* 51, no. 7 (July 2008): 1261–8, doi: 10.1007/s00125-008-1035-7, https:// www.ncbi.nlm.nih.gov/pubmed/18491071.

72. P. Sumithran et al., "Ketosis and Appetite-Mediating Nutrients and Hormones after Weight Loss," abstract, *European Journal of Clinical Nutrition* 67 (July 2013): 759–64, doi:10.1038/ejcn .2013.90, http://www.nature.com/ejcn/journal/v67/n7/full/ejcn201390a.html.

73. S. Pejovic et al., "Leptin and Hunger Levels in Young Healthy Adults after One Night of Sleep Loss," abstract, *Journal of Sleep Research* 19, no. 4 (Dec. 2010): 552–8, doi: 10.1111/j.1365-2869 .2010.00844.x, https://www.ncbi.nlm.nih.gov/pubmed/20545838.

74. S. Taheri et al., "Short Sleep Duration Is Associated with Reduced Leptin, Elevated Ghrelin, and Increased Body Mass Index," *PLOS Medicine* (Dec. 7, 2004), http://journals.plos.org /plosmedicine/article?id=10.1371/journal.pmed.0010062.

75. Elizabeth Renter, "Researchers Link MSG to Weight Gain, Obesity," Natural Society, http:// naturalsociety.com/flavor-enhancer-msg-linked-to-weight-gain/.

76. Sam Montana, "The Facts About MSG and Your Health," Knoji Consumer Knowledge, https:// food-nutrition.knoji.com/the-facts-about-msg-and-your-health/.

77. Q. P. Want and G. Gregory Neely et al., "Sucralose Promotes Food Intake through NPY and a Neuronal Fasting Response," abstract, *Cell Mebabolism* 24, no. 1 (July 12, 2016): 75–90, doi: http://dx.doi.org/10.1016/j.cmet.2016.06.010, http://www.cell.com/cell-metabolism/fulltext /S1550-4131(16)30296-0.

78. Allison Ford, "The Sticky Truth about High-Fructose Corn Syrup," More Lifestyle, http://www .more.com/lifestyle/exercise-health/sticky-truth-about-high-fructose-corn-syrup.

Chapter Eleven

79. J. M. Yuk, T. Yoshimori, and E. K. Jo, "Autophagy and Bacterial Infectious Diseases," abstract, *Experimental and Molecular Medicine* 44, no. 2 (Feb. 29, 2012): 99–108, doi: 10.3858/emm .2012.44.2.032, https://www.ncbi.nlm.nih.gov/pubmed/22257885.

80. A. Paoli et al., "Beyond Weight Loss."

Chapter Twelve
81. Paul Grasgruber et al., "Food Consumption and the Actual Statistics."

Chapter Thirteen
82. "BPA Changes Hormones that Control Puberty, Ovulation," Environmental Health Perspectives (Feb. 18, 2009), http://www.environmentalhealthnews.org/ehs/newscience/BPA-affects-early -puberty-ovulation-in-rats.
83. Meredith Melnick, "Study: How 'Fake' Fats Can Make You Really Fat," *Time* (June 23, 2011), http://healthland.time.com/2011/06/23/study-how-fake-fats-can-make-you-really-fat/.

Appendix C
84. Michael A. Smith, "How to Manage Inflammation by Eating the Right Foods," *The Life Extension Blog*, Life Extension, 20 Sept. 2011. Web. 05 May 2017.
85. Sources of Selected Fatty Acids among the U.S. Population, 2005-06. Epidemiology and Genomics Research Program website. National Cancer Institute. http://epi.grants.cancer.gov /diet/foodsources/fatty_acids/. Updated April 22, 2016. Accessed May 5, 2017.
86. Louise Chang, "Cocoa Boosts 'Good' Cholesterol," CBS News (March 10, 2007) http://www .cbsnews.com/news/cocoa-boosts-good-cholesterol/.

ABOUT THE AUTHOR

DON COLBERT, MD, has been board certified in Family practice for over 25 years and is board certified in Anti-Aging. He is a *New York Times* best-selling author of books such as *The Seven Pillars of Health*, *Dr. Colbert's "I Can Do This" Diet*, and *Let Food Be Your Medicine*, and has over 20 national bestsellers with more than 10 million books sold. He is the medical director of the Divine Health Wellness Center, where he has treated over 50,000 patients.

Dr. Colbert is a frequent guest with John Hagee, Joyce Meyer, Kenneth Copeland, James Robison, Jim Bakker, and other leaders in the body of Christ. Dr. Colbert has also been featured on *The Dr. Oz Show*, Fox News, ABC World News, BBC, and in *Readers Digest*, *News Week*, *Prevention* magazine, and many others.

Dr. Colbert is also an internationally known expert and prolific speaker on Integrative Medicine, and he offers seminars and talks on a variety of topics including "How to Improve Your Health," "The Effects of Stress and How to Overcome It," "Deadly Emotions," and "The Seven Pillars of Health." Through his research and walk with God, Dr. Colbert has been given a unique insight that has helped thousands improve their lives. He and his wife, Mary, reside in Orlando, Florida, and Dallas, Texas.

To contact Dr. Colbert's office, you can do so via:

Internet: www.drcolbert.com
Phone: 407-331-7007
Fax: 407-331-5777
E-mail: info@drcolbert.com
Facebook: facebook.com/DonColbertMD
Twitter: @DonColbert

ALSO FROM DR. COLBERT

NEW YORK TIMES BESTSELLER

Now Includes a 21-Day Meal Plan

DON COLBERT, MD

LET FOOD BE YOUR MEDICINE

DIETARY CHANGES PROVEN TO
PREVENT OR REVERSE DISEASE

ISBN: 978-1-61795-865-6

IF YOU ENJOYED THIS BOOK, WILL YOU CONSIDER SHARING THE MESSAGE WITH OTHERS?

Mention the book in a blog post or through Facebook, Twitter, Pinterest, or upload a picture through Instagram.

Recommend this book to those in your small group, book club, workplace, and classes.

Head over to facebook.com/DonColbertMD, "LIKE" the page, and post a comment as to what you enjoyed the most.

Tweet "I recommend reading #KetoZoneDiet by @DonColbert // @worthypub"

Pick up a copy for someone you know who would be challenged and encouraged by this message.

Write a book review online.

Visit us at worthypublishing.com

twitter.com/worthypub

worthypub.tumblr.com

facebook.com/worthypublishing

pinterest.com/worthypub

instagram.com/worthypub

youtube.com/worthypublishing